World War I
in
POST-
CARDS

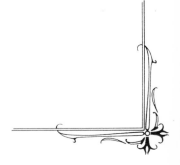

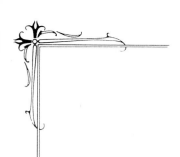

By the Same Author

Military
Middle East Journey
Return to Glory
One Man's War
The Walking Wounded
Digger (The Story of the Australian Soldier)
Scotland the Brave (The Story of the Scottish Soldier)
Jackboot (The Story of the German Soldier)
Tommy Atkins (The Story of the English Soldier)
Jack Tar (The Story of the English Seaman)
Swifter Than Eagles (Biography of Marshal of the Royal Air Force Sir John Salmond)
The Face of War
British Campaign Medals
Codes and Ciphers
Boys in Battle
Women in Battle
Anzacs at War
Links of Leadership (Thirty Centuries of Command)
Surgeons in the Field
Americans in Battle
Letters From the Front 1914–18
The French Foreign Legion
Damn the Dardanelles! (The Story of Gallipoli)
The Australian Army at War 1899–1975
The Arab Armies of the Middle East Wars 1948–1973
The Israeli Army in the Middle East Wars 1948–1973
Fight for the Falklands!
The War of Desperation: Lebanon 1982–85
The Man the Nazis Couldn't Catch
On the Western Front
Brassey's Battles: (3,500 Years of Conflict)
Holy War (Islam Fights)
War Annual 1
War Annual 2
Battlefield Archaeology
Western Front 1916–17 – The Price of Honour
Western Front 1917–18 – The Cost of Victory
Greece, Crete & Syvia 1941: Three Campaigns in Four Months

General
The Hunger to Come (Food and Population Crises)
New Geography 1966–67
New Geography 1968–69
New Geography 1970–71
Anatomy of Captivity (Political Prisoners)
Devil's Goad
Fedayeen (The Arab–Israeli Dilemma)
The Arab Mind
The Israeli Mind
The Dagger of Islam
The Arabs as Master Slavers
The PLO Connections
Know the Middle East

And other titles

World War I
in
POST-CARDS

JOHN LAFFIN

ALAN SUTTON

First published in paperback in the United Kingdom in 1989
Alan Sutton Publishing Limited · Brunswick Road · Gloucester

First published in the United States of America in 1990
Alan Sutton Publishing Inc. · Wolfeboro Falls · NH 03896–0848

British Library Cataloguing in Publication Data

World War I in postcards.
  1. Picture postcards. Special subjects : World War I
  I. Laffin, John *1922–*
769'.499403

  ISBN 0-86299-612-0

Library of Congress Cataloging in Publication data applied for

Typesetting and origination by
Alan Sutton Publishing Limited.
Printed in Great Britain by
Dotesios Printers Limited.

For Luka, Dimian, Kirstie, Owen and Erin

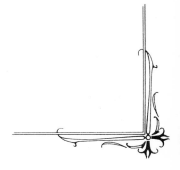

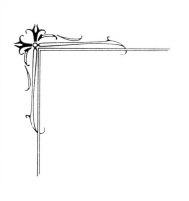

Author's Note

The postcards shown in this book are all from my own collection, which has been built up over a period of more than 30 years. As a military historian I find war postcards invaluable in that they provide me with a greater understanding of the social fabric which lay behind the Great War of 1914–1918.

My wife, Hazelle has, as always, been my main assistant in collecting the postcards and in the presentation of this book. I must also thank Mrs Anny Barbe de Decker for assiduously collecting cards on my behalf in Belgian and French Flanders and for helping me with the translations into English from French, German and Flemish. I am also grateful to Mrs Pearl Donald who translated the Welsh and Dr Rudi Weber for the German translations.

The vast majority of those who were adults during the period 1914–18 are no longer alive. Thus the picture postcards they sent and received have left us with what is, in effect, a memorial to that strange and violent conflict we now refer to as World War I.

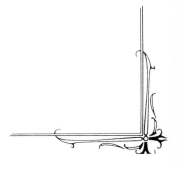

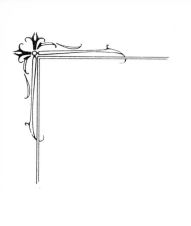

Contents

CHAPTER ONE

The Neglected War Picture Postcard

The Great War of 1914–18, or what we now call World War I, has been relentlessly studied for seventy years. Such close and persistent attention can be justified because of the monstrous nature of the conflict in the field, the political machinations and the social changes wrought by the war.

Historians have analysed politics, strategy, tactics and leadership. Thousands of books have been written about the day-by-day activities of various army units. The medical aspects of the gigantic conflicts have been dissected and described. In addition, many soldiers of all ranks and several nationalities subsequently wrote about their own experiences of war.

That such a vast literature exists is not surprising. The war was fought on a grand scale, with such appalling waste of life and extremes of suffering and sacrifice that it affected virtually every individual in the combatant countries. The war profoundly changed people's attitudes, while at the same time some countries were plunged into bankruptcy and in many nations the basic patterns of society were irrevocably altered. All this has been carefully and thoroughly documented.

The social history of the nations at war has not been neglected. In fact, in the case of the United Kingdom, writers have given as much attention to social history at home as at the front. Yet, 'society' functioned there as well, the servicemen continuing with their eating and sleeping habits, communicating and existing just as their people did at home, but with many more regulations. They lived with many fears, apprehensions and tensions.

Anyone merely glancing at the huge number of books available in a military reference library, such as those in the Imperial War Museum, could easily get the first impression that no aspect of the war had been missed. There is, however, an important thread which has not been followed – war picture postcards. A few pictorial collections have been assembled and published but they are without any serious attempt either to

classify or explain them. Yet, collectively, these postcards were the social currency of the Great War, they were the language through which the soldier at the front and his people at home communicated.

Postcard publishers were quick to see the opportunities presented by the war and there is reason to believe that some already had their designers at work on 4 August 1914, the day on which Britain declared war. Postcards were on sale within three days of the declaration and were widely available before the first troops of the British Expeditionary Force crossed the Channel to France and Belgium. At that time war postcards were only obtainable in Britain; there was no way in which the publishers could distribute them for sale among troops on the Continent. The early cards lampooned the Germans in general and Kaiser Wilhelm in particular. The Germans were 'fat, sausage-eating cowards who would soon run before the stout-hearted British Tommy'.

For a time, firstly at Mons on 23 August, and then at Le Cateau, the B.E.F. held back the German advance. However, the enemy push continued and it was feared that Paris might fall, but as the German army neared the city the troops began to tire and the advance slowed down. The German advance now changed direction turning towards the south, so presenting the French General Gallieni with an opportunity to attack their flank. The French counter-attack was launched in the first week of September along the line of the River Marne and men of the B.E.F. were the first Allied infantry to recross the Marne.

The struggle raged for several days, with the French army and B.E.F. fighting side-by-side. Gradually the Germans were pushed back about 35 miles to the line of the Aisne River, where they turned and dug in. Paris was saved and the war of movement on the Western Front ground to a halt.

Some of the British population, even politicians, still believed that the war would be over by Christmas. Among the more notable exceptions were the Secretary of State for War, Lord Kitchener and the postcard publishers. Kitchener decided to build up an enormous army to support the relatively small number of regulars of the B.E.F., which had suffered dreadful casualties. The garrison towns filled up, old barracks were brought back into use and camps sprang up in many parts of the country. From that point the postcard publishers knew they were onto a good thing. Business was so brisk that the ever enterprising *Daily Mail* produced many cards itself from photographs taken by its own photographers at the front as well as the official government ones. During the first three years of the war – 1914, 1915 and 1916 – the *Daily Mail* probably printed as many cards as all the other producers combined. Most were black and white and while they were not as attractive as the private products they provided a useful commentary on the war.

Many of the early commercially produced cards were light-hearted conversation pieces which followed the tradition of the already vastly popular holiday postcards. Most were little more than a giggle. However, as the war became more ferocious and casualties mounted the tone changed. It was to be expected that the first Battle of Ypres (October 1914) would produce cards of a more serious design. The British were numerically weaker than the Germans and badly led by Sir John French. The Germans were able to punch a hole right through the British lines where they were faced with only cooks and batmen. The British brought in new men by rail faster than the attackers could move forward on foot. Day after day men were fed in on a narrow front, the result being much slaughter and no result. At Ypres alone the B.E.F. suffered heavier casualties than the whole of the previous campaign.

It took the futile battles of Neuve Chapelle on 10 March (13,000 British casualties) and Loos in September–October 1915 (60,000 British casualties) to bring home to the more thoughtful of the British people the real nature of the war. Many others never did understand its frightfulness, even after the horrendous losses on the Somme, with 20,000 British soldiers killed on the first day of the five-month battle.

The postcard producers took the changes into account and employed some of the best war and military artists of the time to reflect the new themes. They included Harry Payne, F. Mackain, Cyrus Cuneo, A. Pearse and R. Caton Woodville who probably brought more tears to British eyes, through the pathos of his paintings, than any other card illustrator. With soldiers suffering the effects of poison gas, and sometimes being blinded by it, there was plenty of scope for pathos.

Even so, very few postcards showed dead or mutilated British or Empire soldiers. Their business instincts told the publishers that soldiers would not want to buy such cards to send home and that civilians would be reluctant to remind soldiers of their likely fate. In any case, the authorities discouraged publication of 'unfortunate subjects', such as dead British soldiers. It was, however, safe to publish cards showing dead Germans, while French ones often featured, in posed photographs, their own soldiers dying on the field of honour and/or glory. The French postcard-buying public seems to have been keen on this theme.

Postcards illustrated the whole range of the intense feelings which the First World War evoked. Also, because the drawing or photograph on each card focused on a single theme the effect was, and still is, a powerful one. In some cases, it is all the more effective because the drawing or painting is a work of art. The main themes are tragedy, patriotism, humour, recruits' bewilderment with army life, the trials and tribulations of active service, suffering and sacrifice,

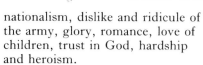

nationalism, dislike and ridicule of the army, glory, romance, love of children, trust in God, hardship and heroism.

These same subjects are echoed in the messages written on the reverse of the cards. What modern historians see inscribed there is sometimes even more revealing about that time than the illustration because each 'message' was written by one person for the exclusive attention of one other person, or perhaps one family. It is, therefore, intimate and at times more so for being restrained, for hinting at that which the writer felt inhibited about saying openly. Many men of that period, especially Englishmen, *were* inhibited, also those soldiers who had received only an elementary education were often inarticulate. The messages on the many postcards illustrated in this book are printed as they were written, complete with spelling mistakes, grammatical errors and lack of punctuation. By correcting the messages I would be hiding an aspect of social history.

These cards were a reflection of the national personality and attitudes of the principal belligerents. French-designed postcards are vividly different from those made for British use, while German, Russian, Belgian and American cards also showed their particular distinctions. Sometimes an artist or photographer of one nationality presented what he imagined to be the personality of an ally or enemy. At other times the producer of a card had propaganda in mind, such as rousing the

passions of his public against the enemy. Many French postcards stress the unity and purpose of the Entente Cordiale – the treaty between France and Britain – and then of the Triple Entente, Britain and France plus Russia.

The primary objective of the postcard publishers' was to sell them at a profit, so they supplied the market with what they believed people wanted. They shamelessly exploited sentiment and sentimentality; among the best selling cards were those which showed blinded soldiers. Generally, though, the producers were convinced that the servicemen themselves wanted to present the war to the people at home in terms of its being a rather rough and uncomfortable game, something which aroused a wry laugh in the recipient. The long series of cards under the general title *Sketches of Tommy's Life* was one of the most successful of the war. Not one of these cards shows a Tommy wounded, dead or really suffering. Here, at worst, life at the front was portrayed as muddy, noisy and tiring.

From 15 September 1916 all new 'pictorial representations, including picture postcards and cigarette stiffeners', which illustrated subjects of a military nature had to be submitted to the Press Bureau for censorship before publication. September 15 was no chance date. On that day the first action by British tanks began. At dawn a solitary tank, D1, under the command of Captain H.W. Mortimer, advanced along the

The Neglected War Picture Postcard

eastern outskirts of Delville Wood. It was the prelude to the battle of Flers-Courcelette, which opened the final stages of the Somme offensive. The Army feared that enthusiastic postcard producers might give away secrets about the tanks, the great new weapon of the war. It was an unnecessary fear; the artists had never seen a tank and had only their imagination to draw upon. They made them look even more fearsome than they were and if any of the early cards which featured tanks had actually reached German Intelligence, the German High Command would have had every reason to be even more alarmed about the fiendish developments taking place behind enemy lines than were their soldiers who faced the monsters from their trenches.

It is perhaps a fair generalisation to say that British cards understated whatever they depicted, and that French ones would overstate it, often to the point of absurdity. German postcard designs were stoical and nationalist in mood. American cards – the United States entered the war in April 1917 – were, in effect, statements of 'Stand aside, buddy, the Americans are here now'. Of course, exceptions came onto the market as the producers experimented with mood. In addition, a good many cards had both French and English text, not only to appeal to a potentially bigger market but to make the card seem more exotic and therefore more desirable. A few cards had text printed in English, French and Flemish, the latter included to flatter the many Flemish-speaking Belgians. Other English language cards also used Russian.

Postcards were enormously popular. Many British soldiers hated having to write letters and found to their satisfaction that a card required a minimum of effort while indicating the maximum of thoughtfulness. Sometimes they wrote no more than five or six words on a card. Even then, the message might be nothing more than *What do you think of this! Fred*. It was an oblique comment by 'Fred' that he was pleased with the sentiment expressed in the photograph or drawing. At other times 'Fred' wrote, *Haven't had a letter recently*, possibly seeing no irony in his own paucity of information.

French soldiers, on the other hand, were different. Writing in small, fine script, they could cram a remarkable amount of information onto a card.

Friends and family at home often used cards rather than letters as they were generally brightly coloured and because they believed, often quite wrongly, that men at the front did not want to be 'bothered' by the mundane details of domestic life. For both the soldier and his family a postcard was safer than a letter because no real depth of feeling or sentiment was necessary. Of course, people did possess very real depths but they were reluctant, even afraid, to express what lay in those depths. Neither group, soldiers nor civilians, wanted to 'upset' the

other. What mattered was to receive a card with a well known or dearly beloved name on it. It was up to the recipient to decode the brief written message and read what lay behind it.

By modern standards of aesthetic, intellectual, political and social judgment, many postcards of 1914–18 may seem naive, grossly over-sentimental, grotesquely distasteful and extravagant in the explicit message of their design. Some can be criticised on a purely military basis, since uniforms and equipment, whether in posed photograph or sketch, are often inaccurately depicted.

Captions are even more inaccurate and the inevitable conclusion is that they were not written by the photographer. The caption writer, with only a few descriptive words from the photographer to guide him, could easily make mistakes. An interesting example occurs on a card showing soldiers supposedly going out onto the battlefield to lay telegraph wires. In fact, they are equipped only to erect barbed wire. It is probable that the photographer would have passed on his negative with the cryptic phrase 'wiring party'. The caption writer, without military experience, used his imagination – and used it wrongly.

Very few people of the time would have been critical of these errors. For them, the cards depicted fundamental realities. They were more interested in the impression than in the fact. Also, people were much less sophisticated about the war than they are now.

They were sentimental because their emotions were continually being stretched; the lack of taste and the extravagance can be put down to strongly held beliefs.

A large majority of people, soldiers and civilians alike, expressed opinions with black or white directness; there were no shades of grey. For instance, it was commonly said that 'The only good German is a dead German'. And, of course, everyone 'knew' that God was 'on the side of the Allies'. The Germans also held the equally firm conviction that He was on the side of the Central Powers. Indeed every time a German soldier fastened his waistbelt he fingered this conviction because on the buckle were the raised words 'Gott Mit Uns' (God with us).

Some British and French postcard artists showed Jesus on the battlefield, helping sorely stricken soldiers. I have never seen a comparable German card, but I have no doubt that they existed because German society of that period was equally devout.

Apart from conventional postcards, the war brought to life an entirely separate genre known as 'silks'. These were cards faced with silk or cotton on which patriotic or romantic legends were colourfully embroidered. They included *Right is might; A present from France; United for liberty; To the victory; A kiss from France; I think of you; Merry Christmas; To my dear mother* (or sister); *Souvenir of the Great War.* Some had a pocket, closed by a flap, to hold a lady's handkerchief. Popular designs on

The Neglected War Picture Postcard

silks were the flags of the Allies, regimental crests and sprays of flowers.

With few exceptions, silks were the product of a French cottage industry and they were on sale in the village close behind the lines. There could have been few British soldiers who did not send home at least one silk.

Throughout the war postcards were cheap, at a halfpenny or penny each, together with halfpenny postage within Britain and one penny overseas. Soldiers paid only a halfpenny postage wherever they were. Their mail was collected by the battalions and despatched across the Channel for posting in Britain. Postcards, when sent by the soldiers from the battle areas to their homes, were subject to the same rules of censorship as were letters. When they were posted within the unit they were read by company officers, but it is extremely rare to find anything blacked out on a wartime card.

It is time to rescue postcards from their obscurity in drawers marked 'War ephemera' or 'Memorabilia 1914–18'. They are historically valuable war documents which, because of their firm substance have survived in better condition than letters. In addition, they cover a wider field than photographs; no photographs were ever taken of much of that which was illustrated by artists.

In postcards is frozen all the sentimentality and the seriousness of a concentrated four-year period which wrenched history out of joint. On a more mundane, but no less important level, war postcards are immensely entertaining and informative.

The postcards of the Great War followed those produced during the Boer War of 1899–1902. They did not, however, establish a tradition as postcards were not repeated in the same way during the Second World War. Relatively few British postcard publishers were active and their range was more limited. The Great War had to a great extent, killed the emotions which had stimulated postcard-buying – sentimentality, innocence and ardent patriotism.

During the Second World War soldiers wrote letters which, it must be said, were mostly dull and routine. When they did send a card it was of the tourist type showing the Pyramids, the Taj Mahal, the Colosseum or some other landmark of the country in which they were serving. The cards they received from home were similarly dull and were generally of the 'saucy' genre from Blackpool or Brighton.

The French, who had taken to picture postcards during the First World War even more avidly than the British, had no 'war postcards' whatsoever during the Second World War. After French pride and patriotism were crushed in May–June 1940 they had no war to fight in Europe. *La gloire*, one of the main themes of 1914–18, was dead. Thereafter, with France occupied by a ruthless enemy it was not possible to produce cards lampooning the Nazis as the postcard publishers had ridiculed 'the Boche' in 1914–18.

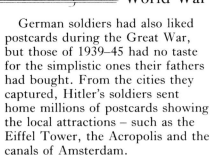

German soldiers had also liked postcards during the Great War, but those of 1939–45 had no taste for the simplistic ones their fathers had bought. From the cities they captured, Hitler's soldiers sent home millions of postcards showing the local attractions – such as the Eiffel Tower, the Acropolis and the canals of Amsterdam.

American servicemen sought out cards of places which they liberated, but otherwise had little interest in special purpose war postcards. During its brief time as a combatant in the Great War the US Army had produced its own picture postcards but the practice was not repeated in the following war.

When the Armistice was signed on 11 November 1918 the event was celebrated with a flurry of colourful, extravagant cards. The Armistice signified not only the end of hostilities, but also brought to a close the era of the war picture postcards. This was a pity. They had brought some humanity and colour to a dark, inhuman activity. They have left a unique link with people of the time.

Author's Note: Many postcards are illustrated in this book. Throughout, whatever the senders wrote on the reverse of the cards is shown in italics. The legend on the front and any printed information on the reverse is enclosed within inverted commas.

The original grammar, spelling and punctuation, or lack of it, in the messages has been preserved. To alter the presentation in any way would be to lessen this book as an authentic record of the time. The punctuation is generally poor and perhaps this tells us something of educational standards before 1914. Sometimes a brief explanation is needed to make sense, in the late twentith century, of something written or drawn seventy-five years earlier. Any such explanations are enclosed within square brackets.

CHAPTER TWO

Laughing at the Funny and the Unfunny

Of all the categories into which war postcards can be catalogued, humour is the largest. This may seen strange. After all, what is funny about war, which is violent, ruthless and bloody? But it is precisely because war is all this and more that men have sought to find some compensating factor. Many soldiers feared that if they did not laugh at their hardships they would go mad.

Captain Bruce Bairnsfather, with his famous 'Old Bill' drawings – which themselves became postcards – had his characters laugh at war. Yet, when analysed, the situations into which he put them were anything but funny. Sometimes his soldiers are joking while being blown up by a shell, whereas in reality they would be badly wounded or dead.

By suspending reality, Bairnsfather makes his characters' predicament humorous. He, and other less gifted artists, appeared to make light of terrible suffering, yet in doing so they were being true to the soldiers who inspired the drawings; *they* made fun of their terrible misfortunes. Two examples can be given here. After a shell had blown off a soldier's leg he says to his mates, 'Oh well, I'll only have one shoe to clean in the mornings.' Another, dying of his injuries, said, 'This is my seventh wound. Seven was always my lucky number – they won't send me back after this one.'

Civilians might have thought that joking about imminent death and persistent suffering was macabre and in bad taste, but the soldiers laughed at it. It was a sardonic, ironic laughter, not light-hearted amusement.

Not all humour postcards showed the battlefield. Many of them were concerned with training which could, in fact, lead to comic situations. All ex-soldiers can remember genuinely funny

incidents which occurred during their recruit training. Had I been an artist rather than a writer I might easily have drawn a cartoon about something which I witnessed one night when walking across a training area in an army camp.

I came across a soldier, one for whose training I was responsible, staggering unsteadily around a circular weapon pit which was full of water following recent rain. When it was dry the pit was the emplacement for an anti-aircraft machine-gun mounted on a tall tripod and it was about five feet deep. The soldier, who was drunk, took a few unsteady steps and dipped one foot in the water. After another few steps he repeated the performance, and so on. Once he lay down flat and plunged his arm in the water up to the shoulder, then rose to his feet and continued with the performance. Bemused, I said;

'What on earth are you doing?'

'Thank God you've come along', the soldier said blearily. 'I've been walking along this bloody river bank for an hour and I can't find a place shallow enough to cross.'

For the soldiers I am writing about here, those of the Great War, amusing episodes took place not only in action and in training, but also on leave, in romantic situations, in delousing baths and when dealing with civilians. Many soldiers, conveniently forgetting that they too had been civilians, came to regard all civilians as dull and unimportant.

Postcard designers took advantage of all these factors, at times in full-blown comic drawings, sometimes in more subtle ways. Soldiers liked such cards, perhaps because they said something which they could not themselves express in words. At times, they regarded the legend on the front of a card as rather more important than the accompanying drawing.

The simplicity of the humour, with its almost complete lack of sophistication is striking. But then the postcards reflect their era.

Laughing at the Funny and the Unfunny

1. Everything else was rationed during wartime, so why not kisses? During World War I this card would have been regarded as sophisticated. It was produced by Art and Humour Publishing Co., Ltd, Chancery Lane, London as one of the 'Now Smile' series. The puns in Holder's Name and Address were considered clever. The artist, Fred Spurgin, was a specialist in this genre.

1.

2. The ambiguous phrasing of this 1914–15 card made it popular. It was innocent humour which would only rouse a faint smile today – probably a patronising one.

3. G.M. Payne produced a series of cards based on training manuals. For him the general impression was more important than his characters' clothing and uniforms, which were always unrealistic or inaccurate – note the footwear of both milkmaid and trooper. The card was sent to Frideen Hughes Esqr., Awelon, St Mary's Road, Llandudno, North Wales. The sender, H. Hl., who was probably a sergeant, wrote in Welsh: *Dear Ebenezer, I have a great longing . . . . This is a fine place also. How did you get on? Best wishes.* The implied great longing was for Wales; the postmark is illegible; and we do not know what Ebenezer may have been getting on with. A frustrating message.

2.

3.

Laughing at the Funny and the Unfunny

4. Drawn without finesse, this card is effective in its message, though only for a soldier. The civilian may see that the centre figure is in trouble from the worried look on his face and the presence of the two armed men, though the cryptic phrase *Orderly Room* would not mean much. The red-haired soldier is under arrest and about to appear before his Company Commander or Battalion Commander in the Orderly Room. He has had his hat removed by the sergeant-major in case he should strike the officer with it and to make him feel like a defaulter. The artist's pseudonym may be significant; in the army a ranker is an officer who has reached commissioned status from the ranks.

Orderly Room.

5. This is characteristic army humour and, as usual, based on fact. In the Great War soldiers became infested with lice and fleas, especially with the onset of trench warfare and its ensuing filth. Mobile bathhouses were set up where the men could have a disinfectant bath, sometimes in great old wine vats. While this was happening, orderlies fumigated their clothing. The artist, preparing a card for 4th Division men to send home at Christmas 1914, enjoyed himself with alliterative effects.

6. Photocrom Co. Ltd of London and Tunbridge Wells produced a 'Camp Silhouette' series, of which this is one of the best known. It makes fun of bayonet practice – which is a serious business with even more deadly intent. Recruits generally found that it was not as simple as they had expected, hence the confusion shown here.

5.

6.

Laughing at the Funny and the Unfunny

7. For the troops, any card which made fun of officers was a good one. That the departing figure is an officer is shown by his cane and better cut of uniform. It is apparent that he is meant to be a staff officer from the soldier's reference to the War Office.

8. Soldiers liked cards which made fun of the bureaucracy and red tape which surrounded them. They were sure that HQ never had its priorities right – an opinion shared by frontline soldiers of all armies. This postcard was probably not drawn by a man with military experience; soldiers did not call sergeants 'Sir'.

7.

" Bit bow-legged, ain't 'e, Bill ? "
" You shut up, and don't give away War Office secrets, me lad."

" Enemy advancing, sir."
" Blow the enemy. H.Q. has just rung through to say that in future all members of His Majesty's forces are to shave daily."

8.

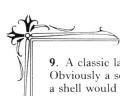

9. A classic laugh-at-disaster card. Obviously a soldier really blown up by a shell would be in as many pieces as the wreckage, but here he is thinking about his cigarettes. Woodbines were the soldiers' favourite cigarette and in an emergency nothing was as consoling as a 'fag'. The famous chaplain Studdert Kennedy became known as Woodbine Willie because he handed out 'smokes' when visiting the trenches.

9.

BLIMEY! If I ain't come off without my Woodbines!

Laughing at the Funny and the Unfunny

10. Another postcard which at first glance seems funny but on deeper analysis is deadly serious. In fact, many a Victoria Cross was won, especially during the early years of the war, by soldiers saving their mates under fire. King George V believed that granting a VC for carrying a wounded man out of action was justified and 'beneficial', although his Commander-in-Chief, Sir Douglas Haig, had told him that any rough movement of a wounded man frequently did more harm than good, and sometimes caused loss of life.

However, some soldiers got off a dangerous battlefield in greater safety by carrying a corpse over their back. This 1916 card may be funnier to the civilian than to the soldier. A bullet in the 'bum' did not merely sting, it penetrated and caused serious spinal wounds. The message, to Master George Hutchinson, 3 Shaw Street, Blackburn, reads: *Dear George Just a card to say, I am improving. The weather has been wet on Sunday and it is a bit showery today. Give love to mother.*

PUT ME DOWN YOU FOOL, YOU'LL GET THE V.C. AND I'M GETTIN' ALL THE BULLETS IN ME PANTS."

10.

11. No explanation is needed for this card, except to say that soldiers, starved of female company, are supposed to be excited by the sight of frilly underwear and night attire. The card is addressed to Mrs Perry, 9 Salisbury Road, St Leonards-on-Sea. The message, with pathos in the last line, is set out in this way:

> *What do you think*
> *of this from*
> > *pink ones*
> > > *The Bury Patchwork*
> *Love to Baby & yourself*
> *Goodbye see you someday.*

12. A card of the Cellesque Series, another product of the Photocrom Co. The words of a famous marching song become ironic in the hands of the artist. The card is addressed in a fine, educated hand to Miss D. Braddick, 'Daphne Ville', Sydney Road, Lidcombe, Sydney, N.S.W., Australia and was written on 26.10.1916. *My dear Dussie, It is such a long time since I had a letter or P.C. from you. I write you a letter + postcards every day. I hope you receive them. I am just the same as always. Are you? With love, Geo. Gray.* The last two sentences could hold a deeper meaning than is apparent at first reading. Geo. Gray is evidently telling Dussie that he still loves her and asks if she loves him. The question appears in many letters and postcards from soldiers.

11.

Laughing at the Funny and the Unfunny

13. Fred Spurgin designed many postcards for the 'N.A.' series which were published by Inter-Art of Red Lion Square, London. This is typical of his 1915 drawings. It is also a common theme and reflects what Spurgin knew to be the average soldier's wishful thinking about female company.

Steadily shoulder to shoulder

12.

GIRLS COLLEGE

FRED™ SPURGIN

THIS IS A NICE PLACE TO BE BILLETED AT!

13.

14. Another Spurgin card for the 'N.A.' series. A simple play on words, as with raw and tender, was considered uproariously funny in 1915. The card was sent to 6 Duke St., West Hartlepool, Durham, Blighty. In the space for correspondence the anonymous sender wrote only *& this*, and underlined it. Blighty was the soldiers' term for England or Britain, probably from the Urdu word *bilati*, meaning at some distance.

15. While this postcard could fit equally well under the heading of *verse*, the artist's emphasis was on humour. There can be little doubt that the girl is pregnant as a result of the bandsman's 'playing with her' and striking the 'wrong note'. A timeless message, its meaning was as clearly understood in 1915 as it is today.

THERE WAS A YOUNG BANDSMAN OF DEE,
TRIED TO PLAY WITH A GIRL ON HIS KNEE,
BUT THE POINT OF THE JOKE IS
HE STRUCK THE WRONG NOTE,
AND THE WEDDING'S ON THURSDAY AT 3.

15.

I'M STILL A RAW RECRUIT —— THAT'S
WHY I'M SO TENDER.
Je suis tendre—je ne suis qu'une recrue.

14.

20

Laughing at the Funny and the Unfunny

16. Tommy Atkins was warned by his chaplains and other officers not to become too familiar with the French and Belgian girls and this card quotes one of the general instructions to troops. Under provocation from the flirting damsels, Our Hero manages to restrain his lust. However, he seems to have found it necessary to cross his fingers behind his back.

17. This postcard, from the 'Valentine's Series', is yet another play on words. With a commonplace message to Miss J. Hughes, Bryn Llan, Bottwnog, Pwllheli, Wales, it was posted on 10 August 1917. When artists drew ordinary servicemen on cards they usually put ungrammatical speech into their mouths. What the men themselves wrote suggests that their speech was poor.

"BE COURTEOUS AND NO MORE!"

16.

THE EVENING POST SPECIAL EDITION
AIRMAN'S GREAT FEAT

hoping you are enjoying yourself
WHAT YER LAUGHING AT?

17.

18. A relatively rare example of French army humour on postcards. The recruit complains to the inspecting officer, 'This is intolerable, this jug is always empty'. The receptacle in question was the traditional French barracks urinal, but the new soldier took it to be a wine jug. Soldiers of other nations had to walk to the latrine block or to the barracks urinal; French soldiers had individual 'jugs'. The card is one of twenty in the 'Collection Humoristique'.

18.

C'est intolérable, cette cruche est toujours vide.

Laughing at the Funny and the Unfunny
SKETCHES OF TOMMY'S LIFE

Between 1915 and 1917 several series of postcards on various aspects of British army life appeared in France. All were drawn by F. Mackain and most were published by P. Gaultier of Boulogne. G. Savigny of Paris appears to have printed some sets under licence. It is not surprising that the enterprising P. Gaultier was based in Boulogne. It was the main port for cross-channel military traffic and nearby, at Etaples, was the biggest British base and training camp. Boulogne was also a leave town, where soldiers might be expected to buy postcards.

Mackain created three series in his 'Sketches of Tommy's Life' – 'At the Base', 'In Training' and 'Up the Line'. He certainly knew the British Army as a whole and in particular the mind of the private soldier.

While Mackain emphasises the humourous, at times he is straightforward and serious, as in his 'Up the Line No. 3'. There was nothing at all funny about going up to the front line, treading the dangerously narrow line of duckboards laid across the mud. One of Mackain's best cards is 'On Sentry Go at Night' where, spellbound and aghast, his two soldiers eye the bombardment. He manages to make the rifle in the mud seem funny but it was another pathetically unfunny situation. This card shows significant attention to detail; by the soldier's side is his rifle-cleaning equipment – oil bottle, pull-through cord, cleaning flannelette – and toothbrush.

The flannelette was known to the soldiers as 'forby', because a piece of the cloth four inches by two inches was drawn through the rifle barrel to clean it. The rum issue in 'One of the bright spots of our life' is amusing; one soldier has turned up not with his mug but his larger mess tin.

Training situations gave Mackain the greatest scope for humour. He made great play of the raw and timid recruit under the fierce eye and tongue of the sergeant-major. In most of this series the recruit is in trouble of some kind. The one which most appealed to soldiers was No. 8, showing Tommy being 'helped' to fire a rifle by, simultaneously, a lance-corporal, sergeant and second lieutenant. Few of these postcards are found with messages written on the reverse, mainly because soldiers sent home sets of the cards with a separate note. One of the cards in this collection, 'At the Base No.4', was sent on 16 April 1918, to Mrs J.C. Matthews, 74 Thorpe Road, Caldmore, Walsall, Staffs, England. *Dear Edie, Many thanks for the letter (reg.) which I received today. I am very glad to hear you are all keeping well as I am in the pink. We are out of the line at present. Havnt heard from Len lately. Love to all your brother Jack.* Jack ends with five kisses.

Mackain's series were popular because they enabled the soldier to illustrate something of his life more clearly than he could perhaps explain for himself. When shown these cards in later life, many old soldiers have laughed in real nostalgic delight.

It's funny how rotten your first uniform looks on you. You wonder how the other chaps manage to appear so smart.

Sketches
of Tommy's life
In Training. — N° 2

First time you got out on the parade grounds and forgot to say "sir" to the Sergt-Major, the man with the big silver headed stick.

Sketches
of Tommy's life
In Training. — N° 4

Laughing at the Funny and the Unfunny

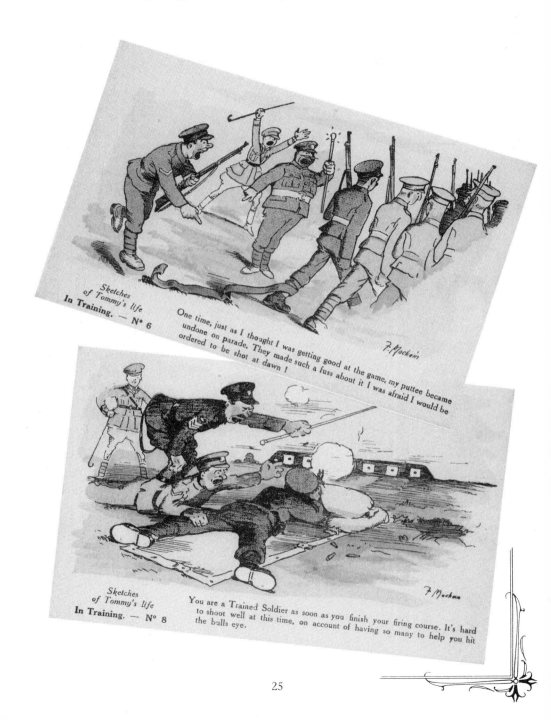

Sketches of Tommy's life
In Training. — Nº 6

One time, just as I thought I was getting good at the game, my puttee became undone on parade. They made such a fuss about it I was afraid I would be ordered to be shot at dawn !

F. Mackain

Sketches of Tommy's life
In Training. — Nº 8

You are a Trained Soldier as soon as you finish your firing course. It's hard to shoot well at this time, on account of having so many to help you hit the bulls eye.

F. Mackain

Sketches
of Tommy's life
In Training. — N° 9

It was a thrilling moment that day, at tea time, when our lot were told off
for the Overseas draft.

Sketches
of Tommy's life
In Training. — N° 10

Naturally, one writes a good many letters describing the many adventures one
is shortly to experience.

Laughing at the Funny and the Unfunny

When I got ready to go to bed, I found I was kindly permitted to sleep on a triangular space large enough to accomodate a small slice of mince pie.

Sketches of Tommy's life
At the Base. — N° 3

You clean your knife and fork by shoving'em in the sand, here at the Base. It's much better than washing them.

Sketches of Tommy's life
At the Base. — N° 2

"House" is the most popular game at the Base. Who hasn't heard those familiar lines : « Eyes down ! Legs eleven ! Kelly's eye ! Blind half hundred ! And another lucky old dip in the bag ! ».

Sketches of Tommy's life
At the Base. — N° 4

Sketches of Tommy's life
At the Base. — N° 5

The new soldier at the Base soon learns that the most important weapon he possesses is his jack knife. He'll have to do most of his overcoming of difficulties with it !

Laughing at the Funny and the Unfunny

Sketches of Tommy's life
At the Base. — N° 9

You might one day put on all your stuff, and say to yourself " It is impossible to carry all this ". But all the time the Q. M. department is getting together a lot more to hand you as a parting gift !

Sketches of Tommy's life
Up the line — N° 3

We marched into the Trenches, late in the evening, going across fields on « duck boards ». There is nothing to be seen but shell-holes, and wintry looking tres.

Sketches of Tommy's life
Up the line — N° 4

The only time I ever saw a man cry was when one of our chaps dropped his rifle in the mud after spending exactly two hours cleaning it.

Sketches of Tommy's life
Up the line — N° 6

On Sentry Go at Night.

Sketches of Tommy's life
Up the line — N° 7

One of the bright spots in our life.

CHAPTER THREE

Military Men

When war broke out on 4 August 1914 most people in Britain confidently expected it to be 'over by Christmas', some newspapers even going so far as to predict as much. However, when the violence of the German attack nearly overwhelmed the French army and the much smaller B.E.F. this confidence evaporated and it became more a matter of *which* Christmas.

The German leaders had put their long-prepared Schlieffen Plan into effect. Under this master war plan, the German armies were to pour through Belgium, which had few modern forts to check them, and first bypass and then capture Paris. The French armies would be caught in a huge encircling movement, thus forcing the French government to surrender. Having been victorious in the west, large numbers of German troops could then be rushed to the east to meet the expected attack from the massive Russian armies. With France crushed, the Germans hoped that Britain, having only a small army, would sue for peace.

The plan collapsed because the Belgians fought well and slowed down the German advance. The French armies, though retreating, were not encircled or beaten and they struck back. The Germans battled desperately to gain a quick, decisive victory by striking towards the Channel ports of Calais and Boulogne. The British army, moving north from the River Marne, blocked their way at Ypres where the fighting became intense and savage. Further north, nearer the sea the Belgians flooded part of the low-lying land stopping the enemy advance. After six weeks of almost incessant fighting Ypres was still in Allied hands and the ports were safe. Nevertheless, there were 50,000 British casualties with the French sustaining equally heavy losses.

Now the armies started to dig in along lines which were to become known as 'The Western Front' – that is, the German western front. The network of trenches grew ever more complex and a pattern of warfare developed. More and more heavy guns came into action on both sides of the front but the immediate battlefield – No-Man's-Land, was dominated by machine-guns.

Few local postcards were available to the soldiers during the first weeks of the war. Tourism was not a significant industry in

northern France or the western Flanders part of Belgium and few shops in the towns and cities sold cards.

The first cards to become available were reprints of newspaper photographs, especially those taken by *Daily Mail* photographers. They showed British troops in training, in the trenches and engaged in battle preparation.

Few official war photographs had reached the front and the *Daily Mail* men, in effect, did the job of official photographers. Many postcards which were stated on the reverse to be 'Daily Mail Battle Pictures' carried on the front the words 'Official Photograph: Crown Copyright Reserved'.

The first cards depicted the many activities of the army and throughout the war this was one of the main themes of postcard production. They showed soldiers in bayonet training, hauling heavy guns, sleeping in trenches, marching to the trenches, at church service before battle, collecting the wounded, burying fallen comrades, and carrying out the multifarious duties expected of fighting men.

Regiments, especially the famous ones such as the Guards, began to issue their own cards. They were eager to show that their tradition of being in the thick of the fighting had continued in the new European war. Almost invariably such regimental cards were in colour and well printed. Photographic cards were in black and white or sepia. It was not long, however, before artists were painting army scenes with photographic accuracy.

By studying a large collection of military-type postcards showing weapons, uniforms, vehicles, trenches and the battlefield itself it is easy to follow the development of the conflict. For instance, in 1914 and 1915 many ambulances were still horsedrawn, but by 1917 all were motor ambulances. From the beginning of the war until mid-1915 British soldiers did not wear gas masks or respirator packs on their chests. The German gas attack on 22 April 1915 changed that and within months every frontline soldier had an issue gas mask.

The constant factors, as well as change, can be seen in postcards. For example, throughout the war most British Empire troops were armed with the S.M.L.E. – Short Magazine Lee Enfield .303 – rifle. The French did not change from their Lebel rifles nor did the Germans from their Mausers. The British uniform remained the same after the issue of steel helmets, though the French army gave up its bright red pantaloons and toned down the blue of its jackets.

Military Men

1. An August 1914 card showing a sergeant, probably a Grenadier Guardsman, armed with the .303 Lee Enfield rifle, the most famous British personal weapon. The Guards used the rifles to such good effect at Mons that the Germans thought they were facing machine-guns. The highly trained riflemen could fire fifteen well-aimed shots a minute and many more if they took only quick aim. The second soldier is using a Vickers medium machine-gun, the mainstay of British infantry defence. The third man is his assistant.

2. One of a *Daily Mail* series of postcards. A battalion chaplain reads the burial service for two soldiers. No date is given but the scene is from early in the war because of the depth of the grave and the absence of steel helmets. Later there would have been neither the time nor the energy to dig such big graves. Steel helmets were not general issue until 1916. The sender of the card, signing himself *Geo*, wrote *With love* on the left of the reverse, followed by six kisses, and *Love to all* on the right, with four kisses. His loved ones may not have been happy to receive a burial scene.

1.

A GOOD COVER FOR USEFUL PLAY WITH A MACHINE GUN.

THE BURIAL OF TWO BRITISH SOLDIERS ON THE BATTLEFIELD.

3. A French photographer prevailed upon a company of Highland soldiers to grimace horribly while making a practice bayonet charge. To any soldier the spectacle is amusing since there would be every chance, in a battle charge of this messy nature, of many of the men being bayoneted or shot in the back. However, the civilian recipients of such a postcard were not critical in 1915 when this photograph was taken. Highland soldiers did not wear their dress sporrans in battle or in training. A khaki apron protected their kilts.

4. The first postcards showing tanks – a strange new weapon in 1916 – were popular. British tanks were used for the first time in fighting at Flers, on the Somme, in September 1916, but despite the caption they were not victorious. They were underpowered and cumbersome, having a speed of less than four miles an hour. Most became stuck in the enemy trenches and in the deep mud.

3. La Guerre 1914-1915. — Bataillon de Volontaires Ecossais chargeant à la baïonnette. Scots volunteer squadron in a bayonet charge. Visé Paris 191

J. Courcier, 8, rue Simon-le-Franc, Paris.

4. A Tank, mud-caked and slightly damaged, coming into Albert after the Battle of September 15th, 1916. BATTLE-SCARRED BUT VICTORIOUS,

Military Men

5. This is claimed to be a photograph but is actually a drawing based on a photograph. Much fighting took place at Contalmaison, near Albert, on the Somme. The caption on the reverse reads: *These 'Tommies' are clearing the road through Contalmaison after its terrible bombardment by our guns.* The inverted commas around Tommies indicates that the nickname had not been completely absorbed into everyday speech and writing at that time .

6. The date is 1916, as the steel helmet worn by the soldier on the far right indicates. The chalk on the ground surface shows that the photograph was taken on the Somme battlefield, where chalk was the underlying rock. Prisoners being escorted to the rear were often used to carry wounded British soldiers. According to the caption on the reverse, the Tommy, spotting the photographer, sat up and shouted, 'Hallo! *I'm* not a German!'

5.

OFFICIAL PHOTOGRAPH.
CROWN COPYRIGHT RESERVED.

6.

WOUNDED "TOMMY" TO THE PHOTOGRAPHER: "I'M NOT A GERMAN!"

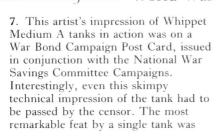

7. This artist's impression of Whippet Medium A tanks in action was on a War Bond Campaign Post Card, issued in conjunction with the National War Savings Committee Campaigns. Interestingly, even this skimpy technical impression of the tank had to be passed by the censor. The most remarkable feat by a single tank was carried out by a Whippet, named 'Musical Box'.

Under Lieut. C.B. Arnold, it fought a solo action against the Germans for ten hours. 'Musical Box' destroyed a gun battery and immense quantities of motor and horse transport, killed numerous German reinforcement troops and destroyed a railway train. The tank was hit and set on fire and the driver killed. The rest of the crew were beaten up by angry Germans but survived the war.

"Daily Mail" WAR PICTURES

64. A BIG MINE EXPLODING.

OFFICIAL PHOTOGRAPH.
CROWN COPYRIGHT RESERVED.

WHIPPET TANKS IN ACTION

8.

36

Military Men

8. This *Daily Mail* War Pictures photograph shows a British mine exploding under the German lines. Photographs such as this, necessarily taken at a distance, were rarely impressive and this one has been heavily and obviously retouched by an artist. It is curious that the ground looks almost unscarred by battle. The tunnel which was dug to plant the mine would have taken months of hard and dangerous labour.

9. Yet another *Daily Mail* war picture showing Highlanders on a sunken road on the Somme. 'Our gallant Highlanders', says the caption, 'who love to charge the enemy to the skirl of the pipes, are fond of playing their national music in lighter mood, as seen in this picture.' Any soldier coming back from the trenches would be in lighter mood from sheer relief. Throughout the war the language of the captions was extravagant. This is another card from 'Geo' and it is dated 24.9.16. On the right side of the reverse he has written; *My dear old mate. These are just cards of what is going on in France. I will send you some more.* Underneath ten kisses he has added: *I am soon coming to give you some real kisses.* On the left of the card appears: *With love to all at home.*

9.

37

10. This photograph of Lancashire soldiers was taken in the summer of 1916 after steel helmets had been issued to all ranks of the British army. It is interesting for its details of equipment. The soldiers are said to be in German dug-outs, but their shelters are not really dug-outs and it is doubtful if they are German. A dug-out was a completely hollowed-out chamber, often with steps and a covered doorway. The positions, which were not in a frontline trench, are characteristically British. The card was one of the most popular with soldiers because it came close to showing the squalid conditions under which they lived.

10.

11.

Military Men

11. By August 1916 *Daily Mail* 'War Pictures' had become 'Battle Pictures', as the great and costly battle of the Somme was then in progress. The caption to this card reads: 'The great traditions of which we were all so proud were maintained, while the individual feats of heroism will be handed down to history' (Divisional order to the London Scottish after July 1st, 1916.) July 1 saw the beginning of the Somme battle; on that day 20,000 British soldiers were killed and 40,000 wounded. Many of the London Scottish shown here would not have survived.

12. In this *Daily Mail* War Picture postcard, a Church of England chaplain is shown conducting a service before battle. Actually, battle is not imminent as these men, unarmed and without equipment, were in a back area. This was another card which appealed to people at home.

CHURCH SERVICE BEFORE BATTLE.

13. The caption on the reverse of this card reads: 'Every British trench is its own post-office, with telephone and telegraph wires. A wiring party is here going forward to its special work.' The caption writer was apparently unaware that this party was going out to erect barbed wire defences and not telegraph wires, which were always buried. The soldier in front is carrying screw-in pickets on which the wire was strung. The object in the foreground is a trench pump to drain water from the trenches. The message on the reverse reads: *Thanks for letter, so glad you have done better this fortnight. We are awfully busy at the depot, three large orders came between Saturday and Monday so we shall have to work hard. No News. Love from both. B.W.* The addressee was Frank H. Waterfield, The House, Cranleigh School, Surrey.

14. The caption on this postcard of December 1916 reads: 'These are King's soldiers and our comrades who have fought and suffered. The best we can give them is their due. Such is the feeling of the devoted Red Cross service.' In fact, the ambulances belonged to the Royal Army Medical Corps, not the Red Cross. Red Cross ambulances were not allowed so close to the front. This is a coloured card, probably to emphasise the red crosses on the vehicles. The message on the reverse is: *Received a letter from you meant for Grandpapa. I have sent it on. Very cold and frost here. Thanks for postcard. Love from both. B.W.*

13.

"Daily Mail" Official Photogr

A WIRING PARTY GOING TO THE TRENCHES

Crown Copyright reserved

135

Military Men

15. Few cards could have carried a more patronising caption than this one. 'One of the queer results of the British shellfire is to provide comfortable holes in which "Tommy" can take a nap after he has captured the ground.' The holes were not comfortable, just a little safer. In any case, they are not shellholes, which are always circular. Some of the soldiers shown here are still digging protective niches, with sandbags at the head, as cover against stray bullets and sporadic shellfire.

14.

"Daily Mail" WAR PICTURES

R.A.M.C. PICKING UP WOUNDED IN A CAPTURED VILLAGE

"TOMMY" FINDS SHELL HOLES COMFORTABLE TO SLEEP IN. 77.

OFFICIAL PHOTOGRAPH. CROWN COPYRIGHT RESERVED.

15.

16. An early French card featuring British soldiers. The front caption reads: 'Arrival of an automobile full of English troops.' The badges indicate several different regiments. The sergeant is from the Army Service Corps. Two French soldiers of the 11th Infantry Regiment were brought into the group. The message, addressed to Mlle M. Read, The Cottage, Ashtead Park, Surrey, Angleterre, is from a French soldier. *Ma chere Mlle Read. J'ai recu vos cigarretes avec plaisir, mais. Je n'ai pas recu une lettre de vous encore. Peut-etre il est perdu. Croyez moi. Votre ami. Sincere François.* (I have received with pleasure your cigarettes but I have not received a letter from you again. Perhaps it is lost. Write to me. Your friend, François.)

17. This is a classic regimental postcard, published in 1916 by Gale and Polden, extolling the glories of the unit's history. Addressed to Mrs Alderson, Hawthwaite, Dent Foot, Nr. Sedbergh, Yorkshire, the message reads: *You would think it funny if I didn't mention about your parcel when I wrote that letter. It only arrived today and I must thank you for your kind present. It will come in very handy for these winter nights for we need something on when we go out as it is awful cold. Yours truly Len.* It would certainly have been cold by 23 November. Mrs Alderson had apparently sent Len a balaclava, scarf or pullover.

LA GUERRE EUROPÉENNE de 1914
144 - Arrivée d'une automobile chargée de troupes anglaises

16.

Military Men

18. The reverse caption reads: 'The Worcester Regiment, whose colours bear the names of Marlborough's and Wellington's victories, was singled out for special mention in the battle of Ypres by Lord (then Sir John) French.' This refers to the Second Ypres of 22 April–25 May 1915. The Worcesters are said to be going into action and as their uniforms are not yet filthy they probably were on their way up. The photographer no doubt said, 'Give us a smile for the people at home, lads!' And the lads obliged. One of them is carrying a mallet for hammering in one type of barbed wire picket post.

THE COLDSTREAM GUARDS.

BATTLE HONOURS.

"Tangier, 1680."
"Namur, 1695."
"Gibraltar, 1704-5."
"Oudenarde."
"Malplaquet."
"Dettingen."
"Lincelles."
"Talavera."
"Barrosa."
"Fuentes d'Onor."
"Nive."

"Peninsula."
"Waterloo."
"Alma."
"Inkerman."
"Sevastopol."
"Tel-el-Kebir."
"Egypt, 1882."
"Suakin, 1885."
"Modder River."
"South Africa,
1899-1902."

HISTORY AND TRADITIONS.

The Coldstream Guards was formed in 1660 from General Monk's regiment which had been formed in 1660, and detachments of two of Cromwell's regiments. During Marlborough's Campaigns it fought gallantly at Oudenarde and Malplaquet, and at many sieges and minor engagements. It fought at Dettingen in 1743, at Fontenoy, 1745. It fought bravely at St. Amand, 1793, where the brunt of the fighting fell on the Coldstreams, who behaved with a spirit and dash which nothing could exceed. It fought gallantly at Lincelles and in many other affairs during the subsequent campaigns. It served in the Peninsula, 1809-14, including the capture of Oporto, the battles of Talavera and Barrosa, and several other important battles and sieges of the campaigns. In 1815 it was present at Quatre Bras and Waterloo, where it had the honour of defending the Chateau of Hougomont—the key of the British position—throughout that memorable day. During the Crimean War it fought with distinction at Alma, at Inkerman and at Sevastopol. It served in the Egyptian Campaign, 1882, and the Suakin Expedition, 1885. During the South African War it is only necessary to say that the Coldstreams in every instance worthily upheld their traditional character of being 'Nulli Secundus.'

17.

THE WORCESTERS GOING INTO ACTION.

18.

19. This *Daily Mail* postcard is one of the most famous of the war, partly because the great artist Augustus John based a painting on the trio. If the men had just come out of a fight, as the caption implies, it was a long way behind them. They are not afraid to stand up, they are relaxed and the houses, road and trees are untouched by shellfire. In the front line 'three on a match' did not apply. Two soldiers just might use the one match to light a cigarette, but if it stayed alight for longer than this an enemy sniper would have had time to take aim. The third man on a match risked his life. Addressed to Mrs Rudd, East Hagbourne, Didcot, the message reads: *Dear Mother, Shall not be home this weekend. Hope you are alright. Tods.*

19.

20.

20. This is the Augustus John painting referred to in the previous caption. The artist's use of ruins as a backdrop suggests a greater battlefield immediacy. Having perceived fraternity in the original group, John enhanced it by having the third figure leaning towards the two lighting a cigarette.

Military Men

21. Another War Bond Campaign Post Card, 'from material supplied by the Ministry of Information'. By 1916 wrecked buildings in France and Belgium were becoming commonplace on cards as a symbol of warfare. An artillery officer gives orders to a gun team bringing a 60-pounder into action. This heavy high-explosive shell caused fearful destruction.

22. Another of the many cards showing tanks which were published following their use on the Somme in November 1916. This one, published by Valentines, leaves no doubt about the Germans' terror. On the far left they are either surrendering or running away. The German officer's cap, left corner, indicates the enemy's demoralisation. The tank is reasonably accurate, considering that artists still had only a hazy idea of what constituted a 'tank'. The tank shown here is a male tank; that is, it fired cannons. A female tank was armed with machine-guns only. The postcard was sent by Leonard to Rev. R. Hughes, Congregational Minister, Uttoxeter.

21.

60 POUNDER MOVING UP IN SUPPORT

BRITISH TANK IN ACTION
SMASHING GERMAN DEFENCES.

PASSED BY PRESS BUREAU
FOR PUBLICATION 24TH NOV. 1916.

22.

23. A French postcard, printed in Rheims, where the city was defended by the Fort of the Pompelle. The Germans were very late to see the advantages of tanks. This one, having come to grief in French trenches, was then hit by artillery and lost its starboard track. The message on the reverse, addressed to Dr Brian Davies, c/o Nell Gwynne, Hereford Hospital, Hereford, reads: *How are the mighty fallen! But we hope that repairs are in progress and proceeding well. With best wishes, Cumminses, Skyborry* [Wales].

24. Another popular *Daily Mail* card. The caption reads: 'These Australian gunners, stripped to the waist, are enduring the double heat of a summer's day and the working of their big gun.' The camera captures the men's muscular activity as they load a 9-inch shell.

23.

2 - Attaque Allemande (1er Juin 1918).
Le FORT de la POMPELLE. — Tank allemand cloué par l'Artillerie française.
FORT of the POMPELLE. — German Tank nailed by the French artillery.

113. HOT WORK BY AUSTRALIAN GUNNERS

24.

CHAPTER FOUR

The Essence of the Man

Artists, photographers and postcard publishers made a conscious effort to portray soldiers, sailors and airmen as they imagined the servicemen saw themselves. Sometimes they did this by facial expression, to show stoicism or resignation, suffering, defiance, cheerfulness or fortitude. A clever artist, such as the Frenchman Dupuis, could achieve much in the way he drew faces and headgear.

Others relied on the serviceman's pose to indicate gallantry, a dashing sense of duty or dedicated fortitude. The experienced Harry Payne, who long before the war had drawn many hundreds of soldiers for various series published by Tuck, used bold, clear lines which instantly focussed the attention of the card buyers on the vigorous elan of his subjects.

The French war artist, Jules Mange, married his soldiers to their background and with clever touches aroused the sentiment of those who bought and received his cards. His drawings for *Le Poilu de Verdun* series, published in Paris by Fantaisie Trichrome A. Noyer, were immensely popular with the French. The English artist T. Gilson was economical in his style, but his drawings and brief legends were skilful and effective.

Among the British servicemen, cards of themselves were third only in popularity to humourous ones and to the embroidered silks. Even so, today they are not found in great variety.

While much can be learned from postcards about living conditions at the front, the artists' drawings and even the photographs incorporate a certain amount of artistic licence. For instance, on one card in this section an observer's loophole in a trench is left uncovered, thus offering an easy target for an enemy sniper. Masking the hole would have detracted from the clarity of the soldier's posed postion, so the inaccuracy is justified.

The drawing on the card entitled 'La Journee du Pas-de-Calais' shows a Scottish and a French soldier in the same trench. In reality, this would have been unlikely but the artistic licence seems justified when its intention was to link the Scots and French as allies.

World War I in Postcards

1 & 2. Two of Dupuis' 'Nos Poilus' (Our Soldiers) series, published in Paris by Color. The first, drawn at Villers Cotterets in December 1914, shows a tough old infantry veteran, whose eyes reflect his experience and the rigors of his campaigns. The other is a French flier, drawn in Arras in 1915. This card was sent to Master F. St. George Caulfield, Villa Frankfurt, Felixstowe, Suffolk, on 29 July 1915, by his Uncle Frank. *This is a picture of a French aviateur. There are any number of aeroplanes about. Two evenings ago between 50 and 60 passed on their way to do a job somewhere – They always fly at a tremendous height and look the size of starlings.*

1.

2.

The Essence of the Man

3. The classic cocky Australian soldier – as seen by a British artist. The hat and Rising Sun badge are embossed on this interesting if inaccurate card. One error is that the Australians were members of the Australian Imperial Force, not the Australian Expeditionary Force. Also, the hat band was not a narrow string but a broad strip. The card was sent to a Mrs Stowers by 3865 C. Fairs, of the Australian Veterinary Corps, while he was in camp at Codford, Wiltshire. *Just a line to say we are sending you our photo they are not too good we are looking too cross hope you are well. We are in a Lewiss gun class next week so will have a good time. We have not enough photo to send all the people of the Framfield [Sussex] this time but have had them taken again so hope they will be better next time. From your sincer friend Vic & Eric.* Pte Fairs survived to return to Australia in 1919.

Some Boy!

From One of the Australian Expeditionary Force.

3.

4 & 5. The Jack Tar of Gilson's 'When You're Ready, Kaiser' typifies British naval tradition. Jaunty, level-headed, irreverent and tough, the sailor is ready to take on the German navy single-handed. The telescope seems like an afterthought but the inclusion of the tattoo reflects their popularity. The translation into French is curious because the Britishness of this card was never likely to be understood by the French. The pipe-smoking seaman from HMS *Dauntless* is a study in steadiness and a classic of its type. It was sent to Able Seaman E.G. Roswell, c/o Hamble Post Office, Southampton by Aunt Louise, who then lived at 175 Chingford Road, Walthamstow. *My dear George, Just a line to let you know how I am getting on. I have not yet* been successful, in my new sphere in the YMCA as I am waiting for somewhere nearer home. I am trying to get Doris in one protem she thought she would like to for a short time to try to settle. I am looking forward to the end of next month to see your smiles, don't forget Aunt Edna thanks you very much for your photo and would like to hear from you when able. Last Sun I went to my friends at Acton and stayed till Monday – had a ripping time. Elsie's cough is much better. Still do my tramp around the bedroom for fresh air. Will try and send you a parcel soon. With much love, your ever affectionate Aunt Louise. I have not heard from you lately. Write and tell me how you are getting on. Aunt Annie moved to Sandy.*

4.
Quand vous voudrez Kaiser.
WHEN YOU'RE READY, KAISER.

"I FEAR NO FOE."
5.

The Essence of the Man

6. The verse on this card, published by A.M. Davis Quality Cards, sums up the public's romantic notion of the Royal Navy midshipman, the most junior officer. Admiral of the Fleet Lord Jellicoe, referred to in the verse, was Commander-in-Chief of the massively strong Royal Navy. Midshipmen were often lauded for their bravery, notably at the Landing at Gallipoli, 25 April 1915, when they were in charge of ships' boats taking the troops into battle.

THE SMILING MIDDY, CHEEKY, BRAVE,
IS LOVED ALIKE BY GAY AND GRAVE;
HE'S FILLED WITH MISCHIEF TO THE BRIM,
BUT, JELLICOE WAS ONCE LIKE HIM.

6.

7. This is one of Jules Mange's finest postcard drawings. Inspired by the poilus' courage at Verdun, Mange cleverly used a wrecked wall to give information. Mars 1916 gives the date of the commencement of the battle. Danloup, Douaumont and Vaux were the great French fortresses on the Verdun front. 'On les aura' (Let's get them!) was the slogan of a famous recruitment and war bonds poster. The soldier shows his courageous defiance by writing in blood on the wall. His uniform and equipment are shown to perfection and he wears two decorations, the Medaille Militaire and the Croix de Guerre. This is one of the very few French postcards without a legend on the front.

8. A Feldpostkorrespondenzkarte or Taboriposta-levelezolap for soldiers of the Austrian-Hungarian armies, published for Christmas 1915. The soldier, having received a parcel from home, is writing to his family while cooking a meal. The curved object pointing towards his pocket is a long-stemmed pipe, much favoured by the German and Austrian-Hungarian troops. The patriotic element is shown by the portrait of Emperor Franz Josef on the wall of the billet. The hunting lodge atmosphere was a popular idea in ordinary Austrian postcards and found its way into military-type cards.

7.

1915

The Essence of the Man

9. A typical Harry Payne up-and-at-'em drawing, this time of the 6th Dragoon Guards or Carabiniers. The card was published by Tuck either in 1914 or the earlier part of 1915. When steel helmets were issued even the cavalry had to change their caps for them. Horsemen were not able to do much 'scouting in the early morning' once the battle lines had become static and protected by barbed wire. It was impossible for a horse to get through or across the barbed wire and trenches and in any case a horse was a large target for enemy riflemen and machine-gunners.

10. A popular *Daily Mail* postcard, perhaps because it showed something of the danger of war without any of its real squalor and hardship. It is accurate in all respects except one. From the enemy trenches the loophole would have stood out sharply inviting a sniper's attention. Such holes were usually covered with sacking which the sentry draped over his head and shoulders. The picture shows a lot of the gear which soldiers had to hang on themselves.

10.

9.

KEEPING A SHARP LOOKOUT
140
Crown Copyright reserved

"Daily Mail"
Official Photograph

11. A French artist's impression of British troops in the front line in Flanders. The card was published in London and Paris. The spirit of wife and child was of characteristically French design. Militarily, the drawing is interesting because it shows well constructed breastworks. Since it was impossible to dig deep trenches in the flat, waterlogged Flemish countryside, the defences were built up above the ground. The sword hanging on the wall of the shelter shows that one of the soldiers was an officer. A sentry peers over No-Man's-Land, which was apparently fairly wide here as the lantern's glow would have been visible from even a short distance.

12. British understatement at work here in both the drawing and caption. This ship was in the middle of an action, as the splash of a near-hit shows. Six-inch shells and their driving charges were coming up from the magazine below decks. This Cyrus Cuneo card was drawn for the War Seal Foundation, whose aim was 'to erect dwellings wherein the disabled service man can live upon his pension and keep his family Without any Appeal to Charity'. The reverse carries the sticker DISABLED 1914–15 SERVICE and the card was priced at a halfpenny.

11.

12.

To the dear ones at home.
Aux chers absents.

THE NAVY IS ACTIVE

The Essence of the Man

13. This drawing of a French and Scottish soldier in a front trench is almost of the Entente Cordiale type but lacks the sentimentality of that genre. It represents a scene in the Pas-de-Calais region, northern France. It was sent on 19 August 1916 to Mrs R. Nock, 48 Bromford Lane, West Bromwich, Staffordshire. *Dear Wife, I have received your Parcel this morning safe thanks very much for it hope you get my letter in good Health Hoping this will find you and Elsie the same I remain your Loving Husband Fred.*

14. From this *Daily Mail* postcard it would have been easy for people at home to get the impression that war was all fun and games, no rougher than a vigorous game of rugby. On the reverse the caption appears as: 'The possession of a German helmet delights "Tommy" and such trophies have become very common in the Big Push. Several are worn by these smiling troops.' The Big Push refers to the Allied offensive which began on 1 July 1916. The 20,000 British soldiers killed on that day and the other 40,000 wounded were not among those left smiling. Several of the men shown here are carrying captured German bayonets.

13.

La Journée du Pas-de-Calais   a. Mayeur.
aout 1916

HAPPY "TOMMIES" WEARING HUN HELMETS

14.

15. This card was one of the most simple and direct of the war. Its straightforward approach to British national pride was calculated to appeal both to servicemen and to civilians.

During World War I the British bulldog and the flag were emotive symbols. The card was one of the 'W.B. Series' published in 1915.

WHAT IS OUR OWN WE'LL HOLD.

15.

16. Postcard producers were eager to show the king at the front and Army GHQ was ready to oblige by providing access to photographers. The king, who liked to be seen in the battle areas, knew that his photograph in the newspapers was good for morale. In fact, he was never taken close to the front, despite the caption on the card. A chance shell could have killed him as readily as any soldier and his loss would have been a devastating blow to the national morale. The absence of steel helmets and the immaculate condition of the king's boots show that he had been taken to a safe position. The officer at rear can be seen to be carrying his overcoat.

THE KING AT THE FRONT.
Crown Copyright reserved

16.

Outside a captured German dug-out
95
"Daily Mail"
Official Photograph

CHAPTER FIVE

Hating, and Laughing at, the Enemy

The soldiers of Britain and its Empire rarely called their German and Austrian-Hungarian enemies by their national name. Mostly they were known as the Boche, a word meaning squarehead, which had been invented by the French. They also commonly referred to the Germans and their allies as Fritz, which was seen as a comic word, and as Jerry, because the German steel helmet looked like a jerry or chamber pot.

It was the propagandists who brought the epithet Hun into the war's vocabulary. It was the most abusive word of all because it likened the Germans of Kaiser Wilhelm's time to the fierce Mongol people who had entered European history in the fourth century. They occupied Germanic territory and for centuries had a reputation for cruelty and barbaric destructiveness. British troops quickly picked up the term Huns and used it when they felt

especially resentful towards the German soldiers, but it was a secondary label to Jerry and Boche.

Many postcard publishers had seen, early in the war, that the Germans could be exploited on cards. But should they be treated as figures of fun or shown as beasts, as the official propagandists desired? The publishers came down heavily in favour of poking fun at Fritz. To do this they urged their artists to make use of all the stereotypes already known to the great British public.

It was widely believed that the Germans drank a lot of beer and ate large amounts of sausage and were consequently grossly fat. There was also an odd belief held by many that the great majority of Germans wore spectacles and sported spiky moustaches. Also that they spoke broken English, using words such as haf (have), den (then), vill (will) and peeg (pig) as in 'peegdog Englander'. They were

supposed to frequently utter the words or phrases' 'Mein Gott!', 'Himmel' or 'Gott in Himmel!' and 'Kamarad!' (Surrender). All these images were used liberally in postcard design.

Even after the German soldier had shown himself to be a formidable adversary, postcard artists persisted in representing him as an incompetent, overweight coward who would quickly surrender to the British and French.

The propagandists, who were at first disappointed that the card producers did not show the Germans as baby-bayoneting Huns, soon accepted the comic image. If the British public saw the Germans as military buffoons there would not be too great a reluctance on the part of the young men to join the army to fight him. The next best thing to hate, for the propagandists, was ridicule.

Postcards of this type were more readily available in Britain than across the Channel behind the Western Front. They sold in large numbers in garrison towns all over the country and astute publishers found a simple way to appeal to the tastes of individual regiments and even of single battalions. They used the name of the unit on the card.

Other types of British postcard drawings were often of a high quality. This was not true, however, of the Boche cards, which were simple and without finesse. French ones referring to the Boche showed more variety, some to the point of crudity.

Hating, and Laughing at, the Enemy

1. The firm of E. Mack of Hampstead, London, sold this and other postcards, substituting various battalions for the 4th Welsh, throughout 1914 and 1915. The bloated, jackbooted Boche simply could not stand up to British cold steel. The card was posted on 11 August 1915 to Miss Cisse & Emily Sendell, 73 City Road, Roath, Cardiff, S. Wales. *Dear All Glad to tell you I am coming down 3 Saturdays from now. I am down for 4 days home Well none of you answered if you had your Broches all right Well remember me to all Very poorly today hope Dad is a little better With Best Love Bert.*

2. Salmon, a postcard producer from Sevenoaks, Kent, also used the cowardly Boche theme. This card was aimed at Members of the Honourable Artillery Company as buyers, but any regiment could be substituted. It was posted on 7 December 1915 to Mrs L. Holt, The Nook, Dinas Terrace, Aberystwyth, Wales. *Dear Aunty, Will be at Euston on Friday to meet you without fail. Bert.*

1.

Hurrah for the 4th WELSH !

If der H. A. C. haf gone by, den I kan kom out.

2.

World War I in Postcards

3: Sticking bayonets in Germans was easy and great fun when they were so fat and frightened. The artist, Donald McGill, played on a military phrase which often appeared in communiques in 1915–16 – 'operations on an extended front'. The card was published by Inter-Art Company, London, in its Twelve-Seven Four Series. The pencil message on the reverse is brief. *What do you think of this for Sunday afternoon sport. Fred.*

4. Kaiser Wilhelm, the German monarch, was frequently shown as a figure of fun on postcards, while propagandists simultaneously depicted him as a new and even more cruel Attila. The German armies were fighting to reach the Channel ports, so the artist of this 1914 card showed what would happen to the Kaiser if he tried to capture Calais. The British and the French would use the boot. The identity of the third ally on the left is puzzling but he was probably Belgian.

3.

WAR NOTE :—
THE BRITISH FORCE IS NOW OPERATING ON AN 'EXTENDED FRONT'.
Nouvelles de la guerre:
Les forces britanniques opèrent sur un front plus étendu

Hating, and Laughing at, the Enemy

5. Bruce Bairnsfather's battlefront cartoons were quickly produced as postcards. This 1916 drawing gave both sender and recipient the satisfaction of knowing that yet another portly Boche was about to be shot. The artist plays upon a well-known phrase put into the mouths of Germans – 'Gott strafe England!' Posted in November, at Barking, Essex, the card was sent to Able Seaman J. Dearn, H.M. Gunboat Excellent, c/o Naval Mail Officer, Dover. *Dear Antony, Many thanks for the pretty card. Hope to see you soon. Agnes.*

Kaiser Bill went up the Hill,
Breathing fire and slaughter,
He'll come down, Without his crown
And so the bounder ought'er.

4.

5.

Bystander copyright

"GOTT STRAFE THIS BARBED WIRE"

6. By day or by night, the dim-witted, rotund enemy was no match for the intrepid Tommy trench-raider. The artist shows him using the carrot and stick approach or, in this case, bayonet and sausage. No publisher's name is shown but we are assured on the reverse that the card is of 'Entirely British Manufacture'.

7. The first use by the British of tanks in battle, in September 1916, was so quickly seized upon by the C.C. Company that they had to seek official approval to publish drawings of the new weapon. In fact, no tank ever looked like this one, which was so frightful that it incorporated Boche-crushing pincers at the front. Those Germans who were not crushed would either run away in panic or surrender. The tanks, which had a speed of only 3 m.p.h., certainly did terrify the Germans although they floundered in the mud.

Now then Fritzey, which do yer like best, a saceage or a funeral?

6.

"THE TALE OF THE TANKS." A Story without Words.
Sanctioned by Censor, Press Bureau, October 10th, 1916.

7.

Hating, and Laughing at, the Enemy

8. A rare example of a one-only postcard drawn by a soldier and sent to his sister, Miss E. Smith, 64 Glencoe Road, Chatham, Kent. *Dear E. Just a P.C. of my own manufacture hoping you* *enjoy yourself alright save a bladebone for me. Yr. Affect. Bro' Tim.* The stamp proves Tim to have been a serviceman. 'Save a bladebone' perhaps indicates that he was hungry for a steak.

9. A contribution to the war effort by the *Daily Mail*, whose photographer induced a sergeant of the Royal Horse Artillery to pose with a shell which was much larger than the RHA ever actually fired. On the reverse is a caption in English and French. 'Our grand artillerymen like to address a shell before they fire it. This shell, being of the biggest size, is addressed to the Biggest Hun.'

'ERE! WOT'S THIS IN MY BEER?'

8.

TO WILLIE WITH COMPLIMENTS

122. A PRESENT FOR THE KAISER.

"Daily Mail" Official Photograph Crown Copyright reserved

9.

10. Taken by a Canadian official photographer, this photograph was turned into a postcard by the Pictorial Newspaper Co., London. It shows German prisoners carrying a wounded Canadian along a communication trench. The theme was much used, often to show the dishevelled and tattered state of the German soldiers. They had to be losing the war if they were in such poor condition, hadn't they?

11. This photograph was taken by a photographer of the Belgian Army's Photographic Service and distributed as a postcard to emphasise the heavy German losses in the Flanders fighting of 1917. 'German bodies in a trench near Blanckhaert.'

FRITZ CARRIES IN ONE OF CANADA'S WOUNDED

10.

11.

Hating, and Laughing at, the Enemy

12. The German submarine, the U-boat – from the German *Unterseeboot* – was seen in Britain as the epitome of German 'frightfulness'. J. Jaggard of 6, Dalkeith Road, Dulwich, London, produced this card with its forthright verse and dedicated all profits to the *Weekly Dispatch* Tobacco Fund. The verse found approbation with Emily, who sent the card to Miss Robey, Soham House, Newmarket, on 2 July 1915. *What do you think of this very good isn't it love Emily*

13. French postcard producers resorted to any and every device to mock and insult the Germans. This was one of their cruder efforts. With the child's potty on the German flag the insult was doubly powerful. The sender, however, did not refer to the design in her message, which concerns family matters.

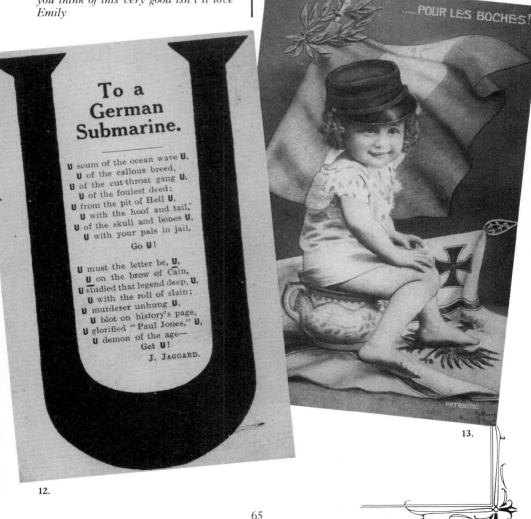

To a German Submarine.

U scum of the ocean wave U,
U of the callous breed,
U of the cut-throat gang U,
U of the foulest deed;
U from the pit of Hell U,
U with the hoof and tail,'
U of the skull and bones U,
U with your pals in jail,
Go **U**!

U must the letter be, U,
U on the brow of Cain,
U studied that legend deep, U,
U with the roll of slain;
U murderer unhung U,
U blot on history's page,
U glorified "Paul Jones," U,
U demon of the age—
Get **U**!

J. JAGGARD.

.....POUR LES BOCHES!

12.

13.

14. One of the few French postcards which made a serious attempt to depict a battlefield incident. A soldier named Brégère surprised an enemy listening post and captured the Germans manning it. The artist drew the Germans' hands unnaturally large and highlighted them, perhaps to emphasise the larger defeat which awaited the German nation. The card was sent late in 1915 from the Hotel de Bordeaux & D'Orleans, Marseille, by A. Goodwin to Miss Lena King, The Ship Hotel, Llangefri, Anglesea. *Dear Lena, Just a few lines as promised. I arrived here from Paris on Wednesday morning en route for the Dardenelles, expect to stay a few days in Marseille waiting for a ship. Will send a P.C. on arrival at destination. Kindest regards to all. from A. Goodwin*. Mr Goodwin, then, was en route to Gallipoli. Since it appears that he was travelling by himself and staying at a leading hotel he was probably an officer. Even so, he was totally ignorant of conditions at Gallipoli if he thought he was going to buy a postcard there.

15. As the war was ending, a French artist showed the Allies carving up Germany. The Kaiser watches them disconsolately. The legend reads, 'The end of a dream – This is not as I have dreamt.'

UN POSTE D'ÉCOUTE BOCHE
SURPRIS ET FAIT PRISONNIER

15. *La fin d'un Rêve – Ce n'est pas ce que j'avais rêvé !!*

Hating, and Laughing at, the Enemy

16. The British had a different way of saying good riddance to the Kaiser. This may have been a propaganda card from a government agency as no publisher's name appears on the reverse.

17 – 21. A Dutch publisher, Imprimerie Elsevier of Amsterdam, produced a long series of anti-German postcards based on the drawings of the famous political cartoonist, Louis Raemaekers. They were printed in book form and the buyer tore out cards as needed. Five are shown here. Each has a top title in French, together with a secondary message below the drawing. Oddly, the main title was not translated although the secondary one was. The titles here are Le Temoignage des Pierres (The testimony of the stones); La Grand Surprise (The big surprise); Sur l'Yser (On the Yser River); Avant la Fusillade (Before the fusillade); La Lettre (The letter).

Each makes a powerful statement. The Testimony of the Stones shows the religious statues (stones) condemning the Germans for their destruction of French cathedrals. German bestiality is illustrated in Before the Fusillade, as soldiers prepare to slaughter civilians. 'Everything in good order, women to the left' refers to the German passion for organisation, even when arranging to slaughter innocent civilians. In the Big Surprise, the Kaiser – whose features were well known to everybody at the time – is shown as Moses II leading his armies towards the conquest of a hated England. As he passes through the Red Sea he is quite unmindful of the doom hanging over him and his people. On the Yser shows that the only way the German army would reach its objective, Calais, was as corpses on the flooded Yser river. The Letter shows Raemaekers at his most caustic. He has a young German soldier, in serious mood, writing home and trying to find something encouraging to say, even if he has to pervert reason to do it. German cemeteries, to which he refers, were indeed large and as he writes yet another soldier is blown up and becomes a corpse. These cards were perhaps for more discerning, educated buyers and they did not sell in large numbers.

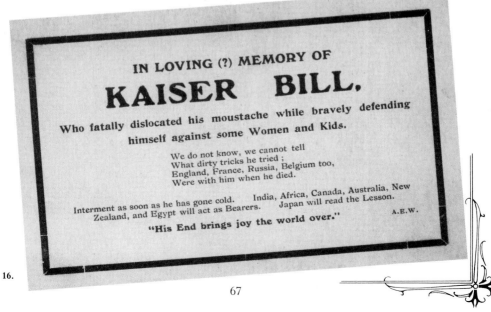

16.

18

LA GRANDE SURPRISE

LE TÉMOIGNAGE
DES PIERRES

MOSES II LEADS HIS CHO-
SEN PEOPLE THROUGH
THE WATERS TO THE
PROMISED (ENG) LAND.

MOISE II CONDUIT SON
PEUPLE ÉLU A TRAVERS
LES EAUX, VERS L'ANGLE
·····TERRE PROMISE.

VOILA LE DESTRUC-
TEUR SACRILÈGE !

HE IS THE
VIOLATOR.

17.

19.

AVANT LA
FUSILLADE

EVERYTHING IN
GOOD ORDER!
WOMEN TO
THE LEFT.

DE L'ORDRE, N'EST
CE PAS? LES FEI
MES A GAUCHE!

LA LETTRE

WE GAINED A GOOD
BIT; OUR CEMETERIES
STRETCH AS FAR AS
THE SEA ALREADY.

....NOUS PROGRESSONS
TOUJOURS! NOS CIME-
TIÈRES VONT JUSQU'A
LA MER!....

20.

SUR L'YSER.

EN ROUTE
POUR CALAIS!

ON THEIR WAY
TO CALAIS

21.

CHAPTER SIX

Women – Romance and Love

It is in the very nature of military life that a soldier probably spends much of his time thinking and talking about women. His desire for feminine company is perhaps heightened by the nature of his life, which, when on active service, is uncomfortable, dirty, disagreeable and dangerous. Its very arduousness produces in him a longing for all that a woman represents to him. During the First World War, soldiers were away from their own country and their own homes, many for the first time, and were constantly on active service.

In the postcards of the time there is no mention whatever of prostitutes or brothels and in only a few is there some oblique hint of the possibility of seduction. But there was much reference to flirtation, romance and love. Sweethearts and wives sent such cards to their men, and soldiers in turn had no difficulty in finding similar cards to send home.

The French seemed to recognise brothels as a military necessity and rarely tried to preach sexual morality and abstinence to their men. The British army did not share this attitude and the generals deplored the existence of red light districts which were officially out of bounds, with Military Police ensuring that soldiers on leave did not get into what were generally called 'houses of ill fame'.

The vast majority of British and Empire soldiers regarded themselves as faithful to a wife, a fiancee or a sweetheart at home – even if they visited prostitutes – seeing no paradox or ambiguity in the distinction between physical relief and genuine feeling.

Separated from their partners, soldiers were often even more in love with them in absentia than when at home. Love became highly romanticised and nowhere more so than on postcards. It is as well to remember, that in a study of romantic cards, the frothiness tends to obscure the very deep longing of the soldiers for their women.

"SOME" STORY!

1. An appealing and innocent drawing, showing a young second lieutenant and his belle. From her gestures and expression what he has just said to her might well have been improper. The card was sent to Miss B. Summerfield, 'The Farm', High St. South, Dunstable. *Dear Lil, Has anything like this ever happened, sorry I cannot come for a ramble tomorrow afternoon, suppose I must be content with a 'Sunday at Home', (some home). Remember me to Mr. & Mrs. S. Yrs sincerely, Cyril.* Cyril seems to have been in camp at Ipswich.

2. Sisters were also important to soldiers, if only because they recalled a more normal life than the army. *Dear Sister just a line wishing you Many Happy returns of the day. From your Brother George. Your gloves are in this envelope.*

A KINDLY GREETING.

A greeting
warm and true,
Speeds its loving
way anew,
As breaks your Birthday
morning once again,
May the long years yet
in store,
Bring for you still
more and more,
Life's choicest gifts
and blessings in
their train.

2.

Women – Romance and Love

3. This was apparently the only card which the sender had available and as the birthday greetings did not apply he crossed them out. The addressee is Miss A. Leuton, Manor House, Bacousthorpe, Holt, Norfolk. *Dear A. Thanks for letter today. Sorry nothing doing for this weekend hoping to see you early next week if all goes well, letter to follow Sunday. Weather fine & warm. Am longing to see you. Yours, love, Sidney*

4. This is a quite uncharacteristic British postcard, one of the 'Artistique' series published by Inter-Art of Barnes, London. Spirit figures rarely appeared on British cards and the incorporation of a woman within the fighting activity is even more unusual. The weapon is an inaccurately drawn Vickers medium machine-gun, which is being fired by an officer.

Though Duty divides us
And keeps us apart.
This greeting will show that
You're still in my heart.

The girl behind the man behind the gun!

Le sentiment du devoir n'exclut pas l'autre.

3.

4.

5. A classic 'Girl I've left behind' card. The thoughts expressed in the verse were genuinely felt by most soldiers. On the reverse, buyers have the assurance that 'This is a REAL PHOTOGRAPH'. Obviously so, but the uniform cap lacks a badge, as does the collar, and the soldier would almost certainly not have been wearing a white shirt. The message is brief but says all that is necessary. *With fondest love, Fred.*

6. This card and its caption supports the generally accepted view that soldiers were keen on girls. The hint of military activity in the background provides the notion of 'work'. The message was written on 9 August 1916 to Miss W. Rogers, The Lawn, Newton near Harston, Cambridge. *Dear Win. Am leaving very early tomorrow. My friend has left Cambridge. Try to see me tonight if possible, same place 6.30. Hope you are well. Alf.* Thousands of postcards were written to arrange a rendezvous and Alf may or may not have been telling the truth about leaving early the following morning. The card contains some interesting postal history. It was posted at 11.15 a.m. yet Alf confidently expected it to be delivered in time for Win to meet him at 6.30 p.m. And all for a halfpenny stamp! Such an efficient postal service has long since vanished.

6.

For a little while we must be parted,
Duty calls, dear,—I must do my share,
Thoughts of home will gladden days of absence,
And I know You're thinking of me there.

A LOVING MESSAGE TO THE GIRL I'VE LEFT BEHIND

5. A.971-5

" All in the day's work."

Women – Romance and Love

7. A Raphael Tuck postcard of 1914, drawn by Ludlow, shows a lieutenant setting off for war. The pathos implicit in the drawing made this one of the most popular early cards.

8. Art and Humour Publishing Co. did well out of Frederick Spurgin cards such as this. It was sold in YMCA recreation huts behind the lines.

GOD HAVE YOU IN HIS KEEPING!

7.

I LONG TO BE WITH YOU, DEAR HEART, BUT COUNTLESS MILES US SEVER, SO SEND THIS TOKEN JUST TO PROVE A LOVE THAT LASTS FOR EVER.

Ever yours — truly

8.

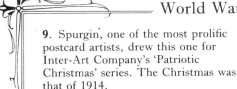
9. Spurgin, one of the most prolific postcard artists, drew this one for Inter-Art Company's 'Patriotic Christmas' series. The Christmas was that of 1914.

10. A card of characteristic French manufacture designed specifically for sale to British soldiers and exploiting the well-known song, 'It's a long Way to Tipperary'. The soldier wears the Light Infantry buglehorn badge. The addressee was Miss M.H. Robertson, 12 Avenue Square, Newinghall,

Musselburgh. The pencil message has faded and is largely indecipherable but it reads in part: . . . . *Its hard times the Tommies are out here are fighting for their lives . . . . Uncle Leishman has done his bit so I am going to do mine now. Mary you can return my compliments to the old woman . . . . Hoping I am spared . . . .* The uniform is inaccurate; British private soldiers did not wear a brace-belt or cross-belt, or a Sam Browne waist belt, as this model is doing.

9.

10.

Women – Romance and Love

11. J. Salmon of Sevenoaks, Kent, hit a winner when he published this card in 1916. It has no space for a message, half the reverse being taken up with ten rhyming couplets. Each of them is numbered to match the numbers of the cards. The soldier sender chose numbers 2 and 9. No. 2 reads: 'As long as the bright stars shine above/Success will be yours and luck in love. No.9: A pleasant trip by land and sea/ With one you love, I do foresee.' He has underlined *luck in love* and *love, I do foresee*. The card was sent to Miss Belldosson, Hawthwaite, Dentsfoot, Sedbergh, Yorks.

THE LUCKY FORTUNE-TELLING CARD.

Choose your Card and you will see
What your future is to be!

11.

POST CARD

This Space may be used for Communication in the British Isles, etc.

The Address only to be Written Here

12 JUN

1.—For duties done,—a position high,
    Will be offered you, I prophesy.

2.—As long as the bright stars shine above
    Success will be yours and luck in love.

3.—Where-so-ever in life you may roam,
    Fond, loving hearts await you at home.

4.—A man who's neither dark nor fair,
    From over seas, to greet, prepare.

5.—A lady fair and of high degree,
    Wishes your very good friend to be.

6.—A fair man is thinking of you to-day,
    He'll probably very soon come your way

7.—A legacy, a cheque and letters, two—
    The ace of clubs foretells for you.

8.—This card brings all your wishes true,
    There is much happiness for you.

9.—A pleasant trip by land and sea,
    With one you love, I do foresee.

10.—Love letters, a gift, or may be a ring,
    The ace of diamonds to you will bring.

R.S.L.   a1602

Miss B Alderson
Hawthwaite
Dentsfoot
Sedbergh.

ONE PENNY

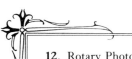

12. Rotary Photo of London assured the buyers of this postcard that it is a 'REAL PHOTOGRAPH'. In the verse, the publishers were catering to the propaganda of 1916. The propagandists campaigned to induce women to urge their men to go to war and fight hard – and they were successful. This verse and others like it appealed to many women who echoed the sentiments so tritely expressed.

13. This card has 'Canadian Official' printed on the front but it is more accurately one of *The Daily Mirror* Canadian Official Series. The photograph was taken in 1915. For the time, the question 'Are they only discussing potatoes?' was sexually suggestive and was intended to titillate. Soldiers often volunteered to work in the fields, especially if this brought them close to girls.

WITH LOVE TO MY OWN DEAR SOLDIER.

Would I have my lover back again ?
Yes, when the fight is o'er—
When the duty's done and honour's won—
But never a day before ;
For I could not love him as I do,
Were he not lover and hero too.

12.

A.398-1.

ARE THEY ONLY DISCUSSING POTATOES?

13.

Women – Romance and Love

14. Arthur Butcher was noted for this type of 'romantic' postcard from 1915. Its double meaning, military and romantic, seems to have appealed to soldiers. It was sent to Miss Cisse Sendell, 73 City Road, Roath, Cardiff. *Dear Ciss Just a few lines thanking you very much for the parcel & I think the photo is very good what do you think of mine it is one of two proofs I had but the good ones I am getting later on Remember me to all. With Best Love Bert.* And Bert sends four kisses. It may be assumed that Ciss understands the point of the drawing.

15. French cards reflecting romance and love generally contained more detail than the British ones. One of the most popular and inventive was 'The Villa of Kisses'. From the bottom up: On the ground floor, 'a first kiss'. On the first floor, 'love without division' (uninhibited love). On the second floor, 'happiness is extreme'. Finally, close to the heavens, 'this is the honeymoon'. It is hard to imagine that a British publisher would have gone so far with suggestiveness.

14.

15.

16. Interestingly, this is a French-designed postcard which uses a British soldier while expressing its message in French only. 'Give me your heart, dear Ange, take this flower in exchange.' It was sent by a French soldier to Mademoiselle Marthe Deluz, Chez M. Lelieur, Hondschoote – a town in northern France. The soldier writer confesses: *Your little heart I adore*.

17. One of the French 'La Favorite' series of 1917. Dreaming of her soldier sweetheart, the typist reads on her keyboard the sentence, 'My thoughts are with you everywhere & always.' Clever design ideas were often copied within the Entente Cordiale but no British postcard publisher seems to have taken this one up.

Donnez-moi votre cœur, cher Ange
Prenez cette fleur en échange.

16.

17.

Women – Romance and Love

18. The uniform in this design could only have come out of a theatrical costumier's wardrobe; it bears no resemblance to any known military uniform in France. The message, however, was universal.

19. Yet another loving-couple design in which the woman's body language expresses reserve. Her arm is across her body and she does not meet her soldier's lips, perhaps to make the moment more tantalising for the viewer. The French reads: 'I wouldn't know how to say it. Very brave and tall I am and my heart is sincere. Tell me? Could I please you well enough one day.' The British soldier who wrote on the card completely ignored the French couple. His unpunctuated message reads: *Well Dear I have not received last weeks paper must be held up in the post. Dear please give my love to all at home I will write to Harry and Hettie as I am on days this week and I shall have more time. Dear Edie please excuse the short news. I think I have said all for now so I will now close with best love and heaps of kisses. I remain your loving husband Fred.* In fact, Fred sent fourteen kisses. This card has neither address nor stamp so was presumably sent in an envelope.

18.

Comme les fleurs, la rosée, mon cœur attend l'amour! 980

As the flowers, the dew, my heart waits for love! Novella

JE NE SAURAIS LE DIRE

Fort brave et grand je suis, et mon cœur est sincère, Dites-moi? Assez bien pourrai-je un jour vous plaire. REX 797

19.

20. The embrace within a romantic leaf was a peculiarly French design. The primary legend reads: 'I love you and it kills me.' Then: 'The leaf will tell you "I die or become devoted to you." The sweetest kiss is the kiss which hides itself.' On the reverse, on 1 August 1916, Edmond writes in French to his 'Dear Fideline'. *Two words for you to tell you that I am always in good health. And I hope that this is the same with you. We are going up into the trenches. We are engaged in the battle of the Somme. I end with an embrace for you and all the family.* The battle of the Somme had been in progress since 1 July, with the French troops engaged south of the Somme river.

21 & 22. A pair of cards featuring the same self-conscious male model and his candy-striped girl. Like so many other postcard belles, she is flower-strewn. The first card's message says: 'Our love has defied pain and death, in order to be able to say one day, "France first!"' There is a play on words here which would be obvious only to a French reader; France being a girl's name. The second card, with its awkwardly posed couple, says: 'Our happiness will be without hindrance! France has set free her two dear slaves.' The underlying message is that after the war the lovers will be free to do as they please.

20.

21.

22.

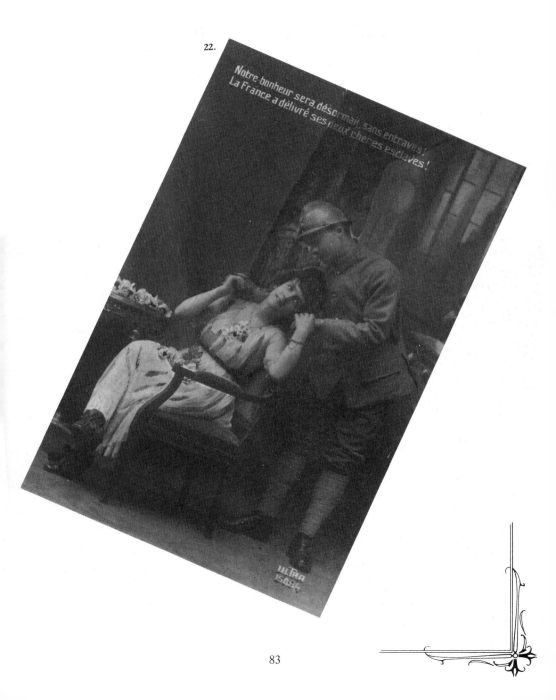

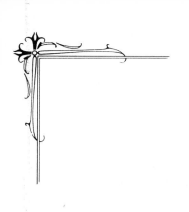

CHAPTER SEVEN

Heroism, Agony and Duty

Since the soldiers' trade is a dangerous one it was natural that they should want to see their courage illustrated on postcards. It was equally understandable that family and friends would wish to see conditions on the battlefield as well as deeds of valour depicted on cards. Many artists exploited this aspect of the war, some excelling in this field. In some cases their aim was to teach and preach; others wanted to arouse sympathy, patriotism and anger.

The artist's range of opportunity was enormous because being able to use his imagination and 'details supplied by eyewitnesses' behind the lines, he did not suffer from the same limitations as photographers, who were rarely able to take pictures under fire. Artists had an extra advantage in that nobody would be likely to question their accuracy. They could depict an act of heroism for which a decoration was awarded, or show soldiers under fire and they could show their desperate plight when wounded.

A soldier blinded in action had profound appeal to the professional instincts of war artists and to the public, perhaps because it seemed to be the worst kind of wound. It wasn't of course; severe stomach wounds, head wounds which exposed the brain and those which left a soldier minus both legs were worse. However, to the artists there was, apparently, a 'romantic' quality about blindness, a kind of military nobility. After all, it would have been impossible to make an eviscerating wound seem in any way romantic. Artists portrayed limp, dead bodies but they never showed blood and in this they were not only discreet but dishonest. Perhaps there were times when an artist supplied blood in a drawing but publishers certainly did not want it. They provided the postcard-buying public with thrills, even with agony, but not with the reality of blood and dismembered limbs.

Photographers took many ghastly photographs, usually after a battle, but these were not made into postcards. However, there was a market for pictures of heroes being

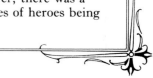

decorated, and for brave rescues under fire. Another popular subject was that of duty, in drawings or photographs. The soldier as a sentry, standing firm and ready for anything, was a popular theme.

Invariably, French artists' battle scenes are more heroic in style than those of their British confreres. British soldiers are shown enduring battle, French soldiers are shown glorying in battle. This applies particularly to Verdun, where the French and Germans suffered about 500,000 casualties each. Verdun was a terrible shambles, a slaughterhouse, but the French soldiers held their Verdun positions which became, symbolically, the spirit of France itself. It is small wonder that artists glorified their soldiers' heroism.

Heroism, Agony and Duty

1. A typical postcard of the Verdun fighting, produced in Paris. The soldier in front supports the heavy machine-gun on his back while his comrade fires the weapon. The 'last cartridge' is an enduring theme in French war history. In the conditions of Verdun this situation happened thousands of times. The helmet in the foreground is German.

2. It is logical that a soldier must anticipate the prospect of being killed in action. Every man who ever went into combat hoped that, if he had to die, he would do so 'decently'. This meant that he would die bravely, his face to the foe, and without great pain. Bamforth's 'Song' series of 1914 illustrated the words of a song popular at the time. However, so many men died as soldiers that the song seemed to many people to be indecent and it faded out. Soldiers did visit their comrades' graves though this was not always easy to do. Men who died of wounds behind the lines might be buried in any one of several hundred cemeteries. Regiments were rarely informed of their whereabouts.

LA BATAILLE SOUS VERDUN, 1916
2 Mitrailleurs, restés seuls, usent leurs dernières Cartouches
THE BATTLE AROUND VERDUN, 1916   Visé. Paris
2 Maxim gunners left alone use their last Cartridges

YES, LET ME LIKE A SOLDIER FALL (2).
I only ask of that proud race, which ends its blaze in me,
To die, the last, and not disgrace its ancient chivalry :
Tho' o'er my clay no banner wave, nor trumpet requiem swell ;
Enough they murmur o'er my grave, he like a soldier fell,
Enough they murmur o'er my grave, he like a soldier fell,
He like a soldier fell.

2.

3. In an early action of the war at Haelem, northeast France, French Carabiniers repulse German Death's Head Hussars, so called because their badge was a skull. Graphically drawn scenes such as this were commonplace on French postcards.

4. A realistic representation of one of the most famous British actions of the war – the last stand of 'L' battery Royal Artillery at Mons, August 1914. It is based on a drawing by a famous Great War artist, F. Matania. Hit by a sudden German barrage, 'L' battery lost many of its gunners, all of its horses and all but one of its guns. This one gun, with an ever decreasing crew, put four German guns out of action and held out until support arrived.

3.

HAELEN. — Les Hussards de la Mort repoussés par nos Carabiniers

THE ROYAL ARTILLERY. The Last Stand of L Battery at Mons.

4.

Heroism, Agony and Duty

5 & 6. Early in the war, A. Pearse drew a series of sketches depicting brave deeds, under the title of 'British Heroes'. One of his first cards showed a Canadian hero and soon after, a sergeant of the Royal Army Medical Corps. Worthy though their deeds were, these soldiers would probably not have received the DCM but the lesser award of the Military Medal had they performed their acts of bravery after that medal's institution in 1916. Pearse could not keep up with the large number of heroic acts and the series lapsed.

BRITISH HEROES.

LANCE-CORPORAL R. G. SHEALE (Distinguished Conduct Medal), 1st Signal Company, Royal Canadian Engineers.
For conspicuous gallantry at Tour de Paissy on September 18 in continuing to transmit messages from a building which was being severely shelled, and remaining at his post notwithstanding that a shell had burst in the room in which he was working.

6.

5.

BRITISH HEROES.

SERGEANT A. E. JOSEPH (Distinguished Conduct Medal), No. 3 Field Ambulance, R.A.M.C. (S.R.).
For gallantry and devotion to duty between October 31 and November 17 in collecting the wounded at night in the woods near Veldhoek.

7. Another moment of French glory as a soldier of the 85th Infantry Regiment, under artillery fire, prevents the Germans from crossing a bridge.

7.

1914. D'OISEAU du 85e d'infanterie arrête un moment le mouvement de l'ennemi sur un pont battu par les balles

8.

"BLINDED FOR YOU!"
From the painting by R. Caton Woodville

8. R. Caton Woodville, one of the best known artists of the war, specialised in this type of unashamedly emotional scene and caption. Blinded and dazed, the soldier is about to pitch into a ravine, in a realistic enough battle scene. The card was sold to raise money for the treatment of blinded servicemen at St Dunstan's, Regent Park. The caption on the reverse reads: 'The soldiers and sailors blinded in this war are "learning to be blind". After their training they go to their own homes or are set up in new ones to carry on the trades they have mastered. Large sums of money are necessary for the after-care of these brave men who gave their sight for us in the war. Contributions will be gladly accepted by the Treasurer, The National Institute for the Blind, Great Portland Street, London.' There was no mention of airmen. Fliers then did not suffer wounds causing blindness as their machines rarely burst into flames.

90

Heroism, Agony and Duty

9. Caton Woodville pursues his theme of war blindness in his fund-raising cards. The blinded soldier is wearing the standard hospital blues. This is a class conscious drawing, since the soldier's 'memories' are all of public school and upper class activities – fishing, cycling, rugby, cricket, tennis, riding to hounds and field shooting. Woodville's soldier, with his campaign ribbons, echoes Woodville's own experiences in the Boer War of 1899–1902. By the date of this drawing medals and ribbons for the First World War had not been issued.

10. Yet again, Caton Woodville squeezes emotion from his public in the name of a good cause – funds for St Dunstan's. The battle has ended and bearers are collecting the wounded. For contrast, Woodville used a Highlander to support the blinded soldier. He rarely made mistakes with his uniforms, accoutrements and weapons.

10.

"WHEN NIGHT SETS IN THE SUN IS DOWN."
From the painting by R. Caton Woodville

"MEMORIES."
From the painting by R. Caton Woodville

9.

11. More agony on the battlefield, this time with a Highlander as the victim. A medical orderly supports him while giving him a drink of water. Traces of the artist's name appear, bottom right. This card was again intended to appeal for funds for St Dunstan's.

12. A Gale and Polden card of 1916 and 1917, showing a Brigade Major with another officer on a visit of inspection to the frontline trench. As required by standing orders, the sentry announces his function. Everything is too clean to be realistic – the men's uniforms, especially their boots, the duckboards, the trench itself. The people at home may have preferred to see this sanitised trench, rather than as it was – battered and muddy and with the troops grimy and dishevelled.

By kind permission of the Ministry of Information

'BLINDED.'

11.

12.

Heroism, Agony and Duty

13. R. Caton Woodville at work again, this time with the Coldstream Guards in action at Martinpuich, on the Somme, in September 1916. Advancing over mud, shellholes and barbed wire entanglements, the Guards suffered terribly but Woodville describes their advance as 'irresistible' and paints it accordingly. This was the type of painting which the High Command favoured.

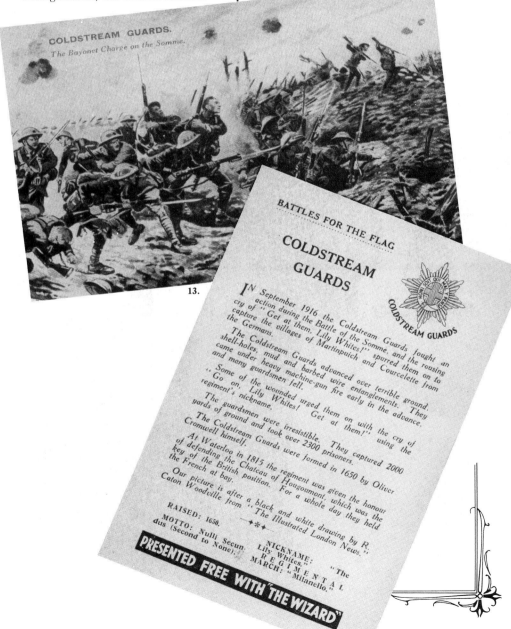

COLDSTREAM GUARDS.
The Bayonet Charge on the Somme.

13.

BATTLES FOR THE FLAG

COLDSTREAM GUARDS

IN September 1916 the Coldstream Guards fought an action during the Battle of the Somme, and the rousing cry of "Get at them, Lily Whites!" spurred them on to capture the villages of Martinpuich and Courcelette from the Germans.

The Coldstream Guards advanced over terrible ground. They came under heavy machine-gun fire early in the advance, and many guardsmen fell.

Some of the wounded urged them on with the cry of "Go on, Lily Whites! Get at them!" using the regiment's nickname.

The guardsmen were irresistible. They captured 2000 yards of ground and took over 2300 prisoners.

The Coldstream Guards were formed in 1650 by Oliver Cromwell himself.

At Waterloo in 1815 the regiment was given the honour of defending the Chateau of Hougoumont, which was the key of the British position. For a whole day they held the French at bay.

Our picture is after a black and white drawing by R. Caton Woodville from "The Illustrated London News."

—★—

RAISED: 1650.

MOTTO: Nulli Secundus (Second to None).

NICKNAME: "Lily Whites," "The REGIMENTAL MARCH: "Milanello."

PRESENTED FREE WITH "THE WIZARD"

14. The *Daily Mail* continued its 'War Pictures' into 1916 and this one shows a scene which was popular on the postcard racks. The caption on the reverse reads: 'A gallant act of self-sacrifice is shown in the photograph, for the man who is carrying a wounded comrade on his back is actually under fire.'

15. Another *Dail Mail* 'War Picture'. A major-general decorates a Canadian lance-corporal with the DCM in the field. Soldiers preferred to receive their honours there, rather than on a formal parade behind the lines. The card was addressed to Frank H. Waterfield, The House, Cranleigh School, Surrey. *Thanks for letter and postcard. D. is much better. Very cold here. B.W.*

14.

50. DECORATING A CANADIAN ON THE FIELD OF BATTLE.

15.

Heroism, Agony and Duty

16. This card was first produced during World War I and appeared again during World War II. The artist was French but the card was published in England in the 'St Clair War Series'. The French influence can be seen in the emotive image of the soldier's imagined home in Tipperary. Militarily, it is inaccurate with the boots, puttees, bayonet-belt buckle and bayonet all faulty.

17. Soldiers' graves rarely appeared on postcards in 1914–15 but during 1916 the *Daily Mail* published several such views. The caption on the reverse reads: 'An Army chaplain is arranging a border of stones around a "Tommy's" grave in a little field cemetery sacred to many of our fallen heroes.' The Graves Registration Unit, which was responsible for the cemeteries, was one of the most continuously busy units. The borders of chalk show that this cemetery is in the Somme region.

16.

IT'S A LONG, LONG WAY TO TIPPERARY.

No. 5

52. ARMY CHAPLAIN TENDING BRITISH GRAVES.

17.

OFFICIAL PHOTOGRAPH,
CROWN COPYRIGHT RESERVED.

18. A drawing of remarkable detail showing a party of Belgian soldiers fighting to the last man. In an isolated house, seventeen Belgians were surrounded by Germans and, refusing requests to surrender, died fighting. No photograph could capture so much graphic atmosphere and the drawing repays close study.

19. The caption of this French card tells almost the whole story of the action it depicts. While the language might be melodramatic, the situation was real enough and even badly wounded soldiers could be inspired to fight on.

18.

Près de Semps. – Une maison isolée défendue par 17 chasseurs est encerclée par les prussiens, sommés de se rendre, les Belges refusent et tombent jusqu'au

1914-15... DEBOUT, LES MORTS ! s'écrie un de nos blessés dans une tranchée envahie par les Allemands, et nos soldats reprennent la tranchée.

1914-15... BE UP ! THE DEAD, cried out one of our wounded in a trench invaded by the germans ; and our soldiers took possession of the trench again.

19.

(E|D)

Heroism, Agony and Duty

20. Short of ammunition, French soldiers in the Vosges Mountains hurl rocks and roll boulders at the Germans. The caption invokes the name of Sidi Brahim, a similar battle fought by the French during their North African conquests a generation earlier. The card was published by Galerie Patriotique.

20.

D'après l'illustration

605

Un nouveau Sidi Brahim:
Les Chasseurs de l'Hilsenfirst

par J. Simont

21. A Belgian aid post on the battlefield. The photograph was taken by a member of the Service photographique de l'armee Belge, the army's own war record unit. In composition and mood, Belgian postcards of soldiers on the battlefield followed the French tradition.

Le Poste de Secours sur le Champ de bataille.

21.

CHAPTER EIGHT

Sewing Silks for Soldiers

Colourfully embroidered postcards, known as 'silks', were a phenomenon of the First World War. Somewhere in a village just behind the battlefront a Frenchwoman probably embroidered the flags of Britain and France on a scrap of silk and attached it to a postcard. A British soldier saw it, wanted to buy it, and a thriving cottage industry was born. This may have been early in 1915.

Women and girls, having found that their first experimental efforts were popular with the soldiers billeted in the towns, settled down to regular sewing. Some women made a steady income from silks throughout the war. In many cases the standard of embroidery was high, especially on the earlier silks. Later to satisfy demand, the workmanship on the silks was in many instances not to the earlier fine standard.

When some of the Paris postcard houses learnt of this market they employed women and girls to produce the silks on a rough assembly line basis. Whether finely sewn or roughly made, silks are colourful and sometimes splendidly so.

Several genres established themselves. The main themes were family remembrance; liberty, unity and right; souvenirs of France and of the war; regimental badges and crests. The selections in this book show all of these.

Some cards were given the additional refinement of a flap which formed a pocket in which a greetings card or a small and sometimes exquisite silk handkerchief could be placed. In nearly all cases such cards were embroidered 'To my dear Mother', 'To my dear Wife' or 'To my dear Sister'.

Soldiers rarely wrote messages on the cards, nothing more than *To Mary from Jim*. I have never come across a silk sent openly in the mail and franked. They were either enclosed in envelopes or taken back home by soldiers returning on leave.

While the women who laboured over the silks were doing so as a business, there was nevertheless

much emotion and sensitivity in their work. A Frenchwoman from near Arras who embroidered silks between 1916 and 1918 told me that a design could take from four to eight hours to complete. She would sell the card direct to a soldier for as little as a few francs, or the 1980s equivalent of 10p. Women working for a postcard producer received a pittance for their work. Today silks sell to collectors for between £3.50 and £5 each.

The Armistice not only brought an end to the war, but also to the production of silks. The French women had made a unique and colourful contribution to the war effort.

Sewing Silks for Soldiers

Sewing Silks for Soldiers

1. 'Silks', or embroidered postcards, were direct appeals to sentiment with their colour, pleasant design and emotive wording. They also provided an attractive contrast to the generally drab and grim surroundings endured by most soldiers. World War I battlefields were hideous, grey landscapes of ruined buildings, torn land and mile upon mile of mud. The sprays of flowers and foliage on the silks served to remind men of home and the more peaceful days before the war.

Personal sentimentality was a major theme of these cards. The legend 'To my dear Sister' was interchangeable with 'dear Mother', 'dear Wife' and 'dear Children'. The makers of these cards understood the soldier's preoccupation with his family and tried to satisfy his yearning for links with them.

2. 'A Merry Christmas' was an obvious theme, as was 'A Happy Easter' and 'A Peaceful New Year'. Again, they were reminders of another, more desirable way of life.

3. 'A Kiss from France' was one of the most attractive designs and was a popular design with soldiers because of its suggestion of a closer intimacy. The soldiers hungered for their womenfolk, and in fact, although they were only a few hundred miles distant, severance was complete. Therefore sending a kiss on a beautifully-embroidered silk was more romantic and satisfying to both parties than an 'X' on a letter or ordinary postcard. Such postcards must have been received with much delight.

2.

3.

Sewing Silks for Soldiers

4. The concept of embroidery for a regimental badge was slow to make its appearance in the designs on silks, perhaps the idea of linking flowers with a martial emblem seemed incongruous.

It did eventually catch on and deft embroiderers incorporated a floral motif with the badge of almost every regiment in the British Army.

4.

5. The ideal of fighting for a righteous cause was never far off and 'Right is Might' was its most frequent expression. A display of the allies flags was the almost invariable accompaniment most to this legend, although sometimes the Christian Cross appeared instead.

6. Finally, silks expressed the universal relief at the end of the war. The Armistice, on 11 November 1918, was like a burst of sunshine to the women who embroidered 'Souvenir of the Great War' and cards such as this were on sale within days, of the signing of the Armistice.

5.

6.

CHAPTER NINE

War and Religion

The name of God is invoked during most wars and political and military leaders confidently assume that He is on their side. Religious spokesmen for the belligerents never have any doubt that the Almighty will give their prayers priority over those of their enemies. After all, for centuries most European armies fought in the name of God, King and Country. During the Great War, leaders sought God's help immediately, urgently and massively. They obviously saw nothing incongruous in asking God to help them slaughter vast numbers of the opposing side, for that is what a prayer for victory entailed. Because of their assumption that right was on their side, leaders did not attempt to justify their request for Divine aid. It was surely obvious to God which side was the evil one.

Oddly enough, remarkably few leaders challenged their opponents' faith in God's help; there were no unseemly arguments about 'God's not on your side, He's on mine!'

During World War I many soldiers had an ambivalent attitude towards God. They expected his help and sometimes they implored him for aid but they also wondered why He permitted so much suffering and slaughter. While most soldiers would go to any lengths to avoid the obligatory church parade on Sundays, many of them prayed privately. While some soldiers 'found' God during the war, others 'lost' Him. Those who escaped wounding during terrible bombardments, who survived serious injury or who stayed sane when they had thought they must crack, found Him. Those who considered their prayers unanswered or who saw all their friends killed and regarded the war as both evil and mad, lost Him. Badly wounded soldiers called to Jesus for help but some reviled Him for allowing such suffering to befall them.

Appeals to God were really appeals to reason. To men at the front the war made no sense. It was so bizarre and obviously wrong that the expression 'God knows' was meant literally and not merely used in a rhetorical sense.

'What do they want us to do this time?' a soldier might ask his mate as they prepared for action.

'God knows,' was the reply, with a resigned and helpless shrug of the shoulders.

'How did you manage to live through that Jerry bombardment yesterday?'

'God knows.'

'Do you think the politicians understand what's happening out here?'

'God knows.'

Religion quickly found its way onto postcards, though more so on the French cards than British ones. In hundreds of French postcard designs angels of mercy float above wounded or doomed soldiers.

Roman Catholic priests and nuns figure prominently in many drawings and in posed photographs. On some cards Jesus Christ himself appeared. Such images were reassuring to soldiers, to their family and friends. It was comforting to know that as a soldier was buried the Church was present to acknowledge his martyrdom. The belief that during some terrible time the Divine Being might intercede was greatly encouraging.

War and Religion

1. Before the war was two months old, a French publisher brought out an 'Edition Patriotique' series of cards and this one was the most forceful. Pope Benoit XV had spurned Kaiser Wilhelm (Guillaume). By extension, this was taken to mean that Jesus himself had turned his back on the imploring Kaiser and gestured him away. The message is that by destroying the temples of God – seen in the background – the Kaiser had provoked divine anger, the implication being that God was on the side of the Allies. On the reverse a French soldier writes to Mademoiselle Blanche Decool, who lived at St. Omer, northern France. *I thank you very much for the surprise which you sent me. Everybody is in good health and I send my best wishes to all the family.*

2. In pose, this was one of the more grotesque French 'religious' postcards. An army padre is bestowing absolution on a stricken soldier. The legend proclaims; 'March on! So much the worse for his grave. Death is nothing. Live the tomb when the fate of the nation is living. March on.' Contrary to appearances, the chaplain is not sticking a sword into the fallen man but merely touching him in a final salute, in the way that a monarch might knight one of his subjects. Most French chaplains wore a sword, which they often used as a form of Christian cross. The card was sent by a soldier named Henri Lofebinc, who does not mention the theme of the card in his own mundane message to a friend.

2.

1.

3. Yet another stricken French soldier dies in the arms of a nun who, with rosary in hand, looks heavenwards. 'Pour le Patrie' – For the Nation – became the official epitaph for all servicemen who were killed. The legend of this 1915 card, 'On the Steps of the Cathedral!' is an exclamation of outrage that a German shell should kill a man as he was about to enter a place of prayer. On the reverse a soldier, writing to *Dear Marie*, confesses that he has been *too negligent* in writing but that he is not forgetful of Marie and her family. He adds a postcript: *My card is not too gay. This is the outlook of the time, which passes. It is beautiful but it is sad.*

4. This card was first produced in 1916 and continued in print for the rest of the war. While it has no direct reference to Verdun, the date, the suggestion of great slaughter and the battle-blasted look of the ground all suggest that Verdun was the inspiration. The burials were attended by the men's commanding officer, the chaplain and his soldier attendant.

5. 'Divine apotheosis!' (transformation); the poilu thinks, as he sees a heavenly vision. 'Beloved glorious flags float victoriously above the battle.' Since angels are carrying the banners of the Allies it is an indication that God is favouring France and its friends.

3.

v. POUR LA PATRIE.

MUSÉE DE L'ARMÉE — Église des Invalides — « NOS MARTYRS pour le Droit et la Liberté »
par JOSEPH AUBERT (1916)

4.

ARMY MUSEUM — Invalid Church — « OUR MARTYRS for Right and Freedom », by JOSEPH AUBERT (1916)

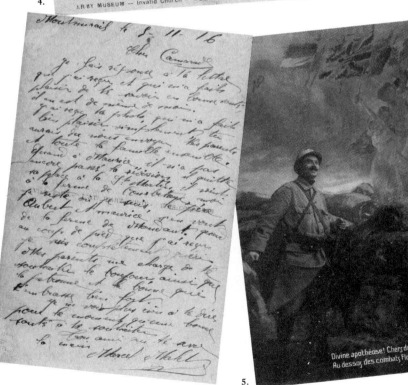

Divine apothéose! Chers drapeaux glorieux!
Au dessus des combats flottez victorieux!

5.

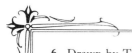

6. Drawn by T. Noyes Lewis and published by the Church Army, this card is typical of those which show Jesus helping wounded men off the battlefield. Above Christ's head are the shadowy faces of soldiers who have already found heavenly peace. The soldier helping his stricken comrade appears to be a Grenadier guardsman. The reverse shows: *One of the C A Flying Squadron has called. Sorry to find you out, hope to see you at the Open-Air Service tonight at 7.45.* Members of the Church Army's Flying Squadron were cheerful extroverts who went into the rear trenches, billets and depots to encourage men to attend the C.A. prayer meetings. This was one of their calling cards.

7. This is one of the most interesting postcards of the war, partly because its exact history is known. The wounded soldier was Rifleman Frederick Charles Taylor of Eastbourne, Sussex. He suffered fourteen bullet and shrapnel wounds while serving with the King's Royal Rifle Corps in France. While Taylor was in Maudsley Hospital, London, the war artist G. Hillyard Swinstead paid a visit. He selected two soldiers as models for the picture he had formed in his mind – choosing them, he said, because of their good table manners. His painting became famous at exhibitions and in churches as a symbol of suffering. Rifleman Taylor was discharged from hospital in 1919 and later owned a shop in Hove. He died in 1965. On the reverse of the card is printed: 'The dear ones at home often say: Jesus, Saviour, let Thy presence be their light and guide. Keep, oh, keep them, in their weakness, At Thy side.' *And especially our dear brothers Sid and Steve. From Florrie. God bless them.*

CHAPTER TEN

Children – Reminders of Home

Soldiers missed their families so it was natural that they should like to send and receive cards in which children appeared. Also, the families themselves knew that cards showing children would be welcome in the trenches and billets and the postcard publishers exploited this sentimentality.

Professional propagandists urged the postcard producers to design 'children cards' which would stimulate patriotism and nationalism – not that these needed much outside stimulation. For many soldiers on all sides the war made little or no sense in political terms. A good many of them had no knowledge of world affairs. They could, however, easily comprehend appeals couched in the language of defending of their own and the nation's children.

Women, with all that they represented, had a powerful appeal to fighting men and they liked to see the opposite sex on postcards. In a way, children were an even more powerful image because of their innocence and wholesomeness. Many women understood the effectiveness of this type of appeal and they often bought such cards for their own children to send to soldier fathers.

The French used children postcards much more frequently than did the British and often in a way which, to the British, would perhaps seem distastefully sentimental. The British when looking at photographic cards in which small French children were dressed in military uniform might say, 'We wouldn't do that!' But we did – even depicting the childrens' military uniforms more accurately than the French. However, while some British postcard series were stuffed full of sentimentality, most were relatively understated. It says much for the Germans' good taste and restraint that they rarely used children in war postcards. Apparently they considered such exploitation to be undignified.

World War I in Postcards

1. This card was drawn by a British artist and it shows a British soldier but the publishers also had the French market in mind, as the dual language caption shows. The sentiment is muted, with only an oblique reference to the separation of families caused by the war. Nevertheless, it tugged at the heartstrings of the time. The card's message was written in French and it was posted in nothern France to an address in Belgium.

2. Some British upper class families dressed small boys in military unforms. Photographs were generally sent to a father in the trenches to show that the next generation was ready to follow in his marching footsteps. This may have been the case here but the back of the card is printed as for a postcard, with the outlined space for a stamp. The cap badge shows the Prince of Wales plume and it may be that of the Cheshire Yeomanry. Nineteen regiments had badges which incorporated the Prince of Wales plume. The chair was evidently used to indicate the small size of the boy but it is also an indication as to the class of home.

1.

"Good night, Dad."
"Bonne nuit, papa."

2.

114

Children – Reminders of Home

3. A card from one of the most famous postcard houses – Raphael Tuck and Sons, 'Art Publishers to Their Majesties the King and Queen'. The Oilette series made liberal use of the flag, children and a standard four-line verse. This card was not sent from home, as might be imagined, but from the front. In its entirety, the written message is *To Bobbie From Daddy. France 1917.*

4 & 5. One of the best-known card series, 'Give me a ticket to heaven', exploited a well-known song of the period. It has no explicit reference to the war or to the military and only two oblique references – the sailor in uniform and the injured man in a hospital bed. The cards were part of the 'Living Picture Series'.

DADDY'S BOY.

I am writing to my Daddy who's a soldier,
And I've told him I am growing big and tall,
And I've said we often pray "God bless and keep him"
And I'm sending love and kisses from us all.

3.

Give me a Ticket to Heaven.
Into a railway station crept a little child one night;
The last train was just leaving, and the bustle at it's height.
The station-master, standing there, looked down with wond'ring eyes
Upon this little maid,—so frail in form, so small in size.
"Where is your father, little one? are you alone?" he cried.   [replied—
With tearful eyes she look'd up in his face, and thus
"Give me a ticket to heaven; That's where Dad's gone, they say
He'll be so lonely without me, Traveling all that way.
Mother died when I was born, sir, And left Dad and me all alone,
So give me a ticket to heaven, please, Before the last train is gone."
105   (*Words by permission of Richard Elton, Denham Harrison, and Francis, Day & Hunter.*)

4.

Give me a Ticket to Heaven.
The station-master said, "Come, little one, I'll see you right.
A ticket to your father you shall have this very night."
He took her to the hospital; they let her see her Dad.
Though injured, he had not been killed, and oh! her heart   [the way,
was glad.
Then turning to that kind friend who had brought her all
She said, "If I lose Dad again, I'll come to you and say,—
"Give me a ticket to Heaven."
106   (*Words by permission of Richard Elton. Denham Harrison, and Francis. Day & Hunter.*)

5.

6. Images of war to complement the main theme, as in this card, were common on French postcards. This one was sent from an Army Post Office on 26 April 1916 to Mrs A. Dalton, Statham Crossings, Lymm, Warrington, Cheshire. The message reads: *Many thanks for the parcel that you gave my wife to send to me and I hope this will find you in the best of health also your mother and father so now I must close with my best respects from Sgt Leigh.* The little French boy, in his 'Letter to Papa', is saying: 'I do not find the word, dear father, in my heart. I love you, return to us victorious.'

7. A characteristic French postcard showing that the fighting man would have reinforcements from the next generation. Flowers were nearly always evident, even if they had to be forced incongruously into the setting. The legend reads: 'France, dear country! Soldiers of the future receive a proud salute.'

France! chère Patrie!
de tes futurs soldats reçois un fier salut.

DIX
115

7.

Lettre au Papa
Je ne trouve qu'un mot, cher père, dans mon cœur
de t'aime, reviens-nous vainqueur

DIX
147/3

6.

116

Children – Reminders of Home

8. Throughout the war the French invoked Alsace in postcards, posters, poems and photographs. Possession of the Alsace region had traditionally been one of the causes of fierce disputes between France and Germany. It was the first French territory to be occupied by the Germans in 1914. The little girl carries the flowers of Alsace as a reminder that they 'open to the light of the sun and liberty'. As a secondary image, a soldier is dying for those flowers and liberty.

9. The simple image of the poilu on leave being reunited with his children was enough to stir Frenchmen into renewed hatred of the German foe who kept them apart. Almost invariably, French children on postcards were elaborately dressed. The card was sent from France to England on 9 November 1915. *My dear Nell. Am sending you enclosed a few flags which I promised you. Am writing you in a few days. Hope things are going all right. With love. Yrs. etc. Jack*

FLEURS D'ALSACE
Elles s'ouvrent à la clarté
Du soleil de la Liberté
Revanche
191

Enfin Réunis

8.

9.

10. This card is highly charged with symbolism, proclaiming as it does that 'France recovers her children'. The 'children' represent the province of Alsace, a territory long disputed between France and Germany. The woman in the photograph wears a Revolutionary bonnet, another symbol of fighting France. In a message of 4 July 1915 which extends to 180 words, Joseph explains to his sister, Marie, how a private code they have worked out will tell her where he is stationed. Translated from the French: *This time I'm on the point of leaving, equipped and in a new uniform, everything brand new. I will probably go to the 125th regiment if there aren't any changes in the appointments. I will write to you on my arrival or before en route if we stop for sufficient time. According to our agreement, the first letters of my sentences will represent the place where I am and other information that we are obliged to keep secret. Do you understand? I am in Diors today. I won't come back here before my departure. It's warm enough. I love you. Your brother.* Below this is a second message to Marie, this time from their father. *However unhappy this makes us we can be glad that he hasn't had to leave earlier. Anyhow, we wish him good luck.* Had this card been read by anybody in authority Joseph would almost certainly have been charged with a serious breach of security and his punishment could have been death. He took the precaution of sending the card in an envelope.

10.

Children – Reminders of Home

11. A simple, explicit and flamboyant message. The traditional cock of France triumphs over the German 'eagle of infamy' and sends it, in its death throes, to the ground. This imagery alone might have been sufficient for some publishers but not for the makers of the 'Patriotic' series. They had to squeeze more emotion from the viewer by using children grasping the national flag. On the reverse, Alphonse sends his dear Leontine an immensely long message. In summary, he says that he sent his photograph ten days before and he is worried that he has had no response. Perhaps it has been lost. He has had too much to do but has no real news. He advises Leontine not to see too much of Victorine and he sends kindest regards to all the family.

11.

12. A 1915 fighter plane – capable of 60 m.p.h. – flies over a tented camp. In the foreground 'Le Petit Français' (the Young Frenchman) announces: 'To our courageous brothers go our most tender wishes.' The card was written on 10 October 1915. The message itself, which went to 'Dear Papa' from his children, is also in sentimental vein. Translated from the French: *We are sending this card to tell you that the whole family is well and we hope the same for you. We hope also that you had a good journey. Your little children hope that their daddy will soon come to see them – and stay with them. Your children are waiting to kiss you and want to do this in reality. We are very proud of you.*

13. 'The Europe of tomorrow remains faithful to the Alliance', the legend proclaims. The children, representing Italy, Serbia, Britain and France, show by their expressions that the experience of dressing up has been a lot of fun. The French produced so many 'Alliance' cards that it is easy to get the impression that they actually feared for its cohesion.

12.

13.

Children – Reminders of Home

14. More costumed children who, the legend tells us, are confident that their father will be safe, with all their heart, strength and hope. The eternal French theme of 'La Gloire' – Glory in war – is never far off. Here the success of a dramatic cavalry charge is assured by the presence of a heavenly body ready to garland the leader of the heroic horsemen. Writing to her 'Cher Demoiselle', a girl named Marie sends thousands of kisses to Ginette.

15. Children posing as a wounded warrior and his devoted nurse appealed profoundly to French sentiment. 'We enter the field when our elders are no more', says the infant warrior. It was just one more way the French card publishers found to say that, even into the next generation, 'We will never surrender'.

14.

15.

16. Another floral tribute. 'Dear father, for thee I have assembled these flowers: May they please you and bring you good luck.' The sylvan scene at home was intended to remind the soldier of his return to a better life. It is noticeable that on almost every card on which a French soldier is carrying his rifle, the bayonet is fixed. This was rarely so on British postcards. The message is brief: *Thank you for your pretty card. Kind regards.*

16.

CHAPTER ELEVEN

Soldiers and Animals

While animals, especially horses, took part in the war in large numbers, they are the central theme in relatively few postcards. Where they do appear they are incidental to the main idea expressed on the cards.

This is strange because British soldiers were devoted to their animal comrades. Animals appear in thousands of photographs and in the work of some war artists. Also, the British army tradition of animal mascots might have been expected to appear on some cards. Similarly, there was a national tradition of sentimentality about animals, notably horses and dogs.

The French were unlikely to produce postcards glorifying the horse since in France horseflesh was, and still is, as important a meat as beef and lamb, although the dog might have appeared more than it did. The only creature emphasised on French cards is the cock and then only because it was the national symbol.

I am unaware of any postcard based on the mule, though these beasts of burden were vital in getting ammunition and supplies through the mud to the forward distribution points.

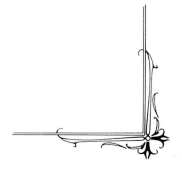

1. The *Daily Mirror* turned this happy scene into a postcard in 1917. The Canadian soldiers' delight was not feigned for the camera. A dog was a symbol of normality in a grossly abnormal life, as was a woman – who in this case happened to be the most appealing of all women to soldiers, a nursing sister. She represented all that the men most deeply missed, from their lives at home.

2. This simple drawing illustrates the British soldier's affection for his horse. It was a tradition, as well as a regulation, among cavalrymen, gunners, transport drivers and others who used horses that they should care for their animals before themselves. Soldiers often had to shoot badly wounded animals to put them out of their pain and they said it was one of their most difficult and distressing of duties. This is an E. Mack card of 1915.

CANADA FINDS A LITTLE DOG IN HUN TRENCHES & PRESENTS IT TO NURSE

1.

Soldiers and Animals

3. During the war and more so towards the end of it, many soldiers brought home their pet dogs. They wanted to keep them but regulations insisted that they first be quarantined to ensure that they were not infected with rabies and other diseases. The Blue Cross took on the responsibility of raising the money necessary to maintain them.

BLUE CROSS QUARANTINE KENNELS, Charlton Kennels, Shooters Hill, S.E.18 For Soldiers' Dogs from the War Zones. Donations towards Maintenance urgently needed. ARTHUR J. COKE, Secretary, 58 Victoria Street, London, S.W.1

Is there a Blue Cross Kennel for me?

3.

PALS!

2.

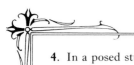

World War I in Postcards

4. In a posed studio photograph a field nurse succours a wounded French soldier with brandy brought onto the battlefield by a brave dog. It is impossible to imagine this as a British card. British war dogs were used to carry messages but never alcohol. The card, which declares 'Courage, Devotion', is characteristically crowded. It shows an angel crowning the charging French cavalry with a laurel wreath, infantrymen lining a breastwork, a gun-team in action and a burning town.

4.

CHAPTER TWELVE

The War in Rhyme

From the first year of the war, rhyme-makers found in postcards ample scope for their verbal skills. They helped to create a postcard genre in which the verse was more dominant than the accompanying drawing or posed photograph. The design merely framed the verse. In ordinary life there was nothing new about verse cards, which could be found in any holiday resort. However, the war increased the flow of the cards and intensified the sentiments expressed on them.

Some war cards were made up entirely of verse, with up to ten stanzas of simple and generally sentimental rhyme. No academic would have called it poet·y but certainly it often portrayed emotion, one of the prerequisites of real poetry. Postcard verse of 1914–18 had no complexities of style or content, but then, it was meant to satisfy the emotions of the people who read it, not to stimulate their minds.

Certain words frequently recur. Among them are pray, which was often rhymed with day or say; duty, commonly rhymed with

beauty; and grief, linked with relief or brief. The versifiers wrote for the moment and the market, not for posterity, so they ignored poetic abstracts.

However, their verses were not without skill. They deliberately plucked at the heartstrings of people who were already in a state of high emotional tension. Many were moved to tears by verse cards, as with the series, 'The Pardon Came Too Late' and 'Sandy, Boy'. Others had their patriotic pride stirred. Yet others found in verse cards the sentiments and love they could not express themselves but which they wanted to convey to their loved ones.

The verse-makers rarely signed their work. One reason may have been that the publishers wanted the buyers of the cards to feel that they had created the rhymes. Also, soldiers would have wanted to feel that the sentiments expressed on the cards they received were directly from a dear one at home, not from a professional versifier.

As the war lenghtened and the suffering of the soldiers increased, so

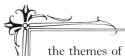
the themes of the verses became more religious. Perhaps the publishers detected a public desire for reassurance and rationality which, they believed, prayer might supply.

All the combatant nations produced verse cards, but most of those illustrated here are in English because foreign language verse loses much of its effect in translation.

SANDY, BOY (1).

"Sandy, boy, the pipes are calling, over glen and mountain side,
Said the bonnie Hieland lassie, as they parted by the Dee,
Duty calls, my soldier lad, buckle on your tartan plaid!"
"For, where'er you go, my love, I know you'll leave your heart with me."

WORDS BY PERMISSION OF THE STAR MUSIC PUBLISHING CO., LONDON.

BAMFORTH (Copyright).

1.

128

The War in Rhyme

1 – 3. 'Sandy, Boy' published by Bamforth, was a three-part tear-jerker, with two of the posed photographs projecting a double image. The themes were carefully planned. On Card 1 the theme was duty, Card 2 sorrow through absence and on Card 3 glory became dominant. Every image was calculated to produce a pleasing whole and both senders and recipients pored over the details. 'Sandy, Boy' was published in 1915 when 'glory' still seemed to be a valid factor in the war.

SANDY, BOY (3).

Sandy, boy, when battle's raging, and there's glory to be won,
I know you'll be brave and true, fighting like the Scotch boys do.
All the time I shall be praying for your safe return to me.
There'll be hearty cheers and no more tears beside the silv'ry Dee.

WORDS BY PERMISSION OF THE STAR MUSIC PUBLISHING CO., LONDON.   BAMFORTH (Copyright)

3.

SANDY, BOY (2).

"Sandy, boy, my soldier laddie, when you're far from Scotland's shore,
Dinna forget your ain wee lassie.
Keep the bonnie heather we gathered together, and my sad heart beats with joy;
I hear those pipers playing, to see the Cameron men,
I'll be feelin' awfu' proud, ye ken, to see the Cameron men,
And my ain true Sandy boy."

BAMFORTH (Copyright).
WORDS BY PERMISSION OF THE STAR MUSIC PUBLISHING CO., LONDON.

4. This verse card, published by Benton of Brighton, was written around a set of cliches and designed to appeal to soldiers who were unlikely to go to the trouble of writing letters. Nevertheless, Albany Tindal, who signed the front of the card in the space provided, did write on the back to Mifa (sic) M.J. Smith, Dunville House, Havant, Hampshire. *There is no word of me going off yet but I am expecting to go soon there was a big draft left here on Saturday night it was a common thing for them to leave on Tuesday but now the days are active. I had a letter from Mrs T she is asking for you & has promised to write you soon if she has not done so Ere this time hoping you are in good health as I am in the top of good form Yours truly write soon.*

"I'm Thinking of YOU Everyday."
At NIGG CAMP. — A Soldier's Letter.

I haven't had time to sit down and write,
And thought perhaps you might grieve:
So I send you this card just to say I'm alright,
And longing to see you again when on "leave."
When the Empire's Call for more men to fight,
For her Honour—in me caused a thrill;
I felt fight I must or else I should "bust,"
So I'm "doing my bit" at NIGG, until—
My duty calls me as this picture shows,
To the Front where the fightin' is done;
And once BRITISH TOMMIES get grip on the foe,
There's no letting go till they've won.
The work it is hard, for we're "at it" all day,
And sometimes half of the night;
But we're hardening to it and getting quite fit,
And thank goodness for "grub" we're alright.
So cheer up, my dear, tho' parted we are,
And though I'm so far away;
My loved ones are ever first in my thoughts,
I'm thinking of YOU everyday.
(Copyright).
From Albany Tindal

At "Duty's Call."

4.

5 & 6. The postcard publishers Beagles of London – who claimed to be 'Best in the World' – specialised in cards with patriotic and religious themes, sometimes linking the two. 'To my Dear Brother at the Front' was typical. Similarly, there were Dear Father, Dear Husband and Dear Fiance cards. 'Greetings From Home' was a standard central legend, as was the use of King George V portrait. The message on the reverse of this card is simplicity itself. *From all at home with good wishes. J. Cox From your loveing wife Kate Cox.*

The War in Rhyme

TO MY DEAR BROTHER AT THE FRONT.

GOD BRING YOU
SAFELY BACK AGAIN
TO THOSE WHO HOLD YOU DEAR,
GOD KEEP YOU FREE FROM HARM & PAIN. WHEN DANGER LURKETH NEAR.
THOUGH FAR AWAY FROM THOSE YOU LOVE
MAY HE SUPPLY EACH NEED,
GIVE STRENGTH & COURAGE FROM ABOVE, SUCCESS, GOOD LUCK, GODSPEED.

COPYRIGHT   BEAGLES POSTCARDS

5.

GREETINGS FROM HOME.

WE'RE
ALL OF US
THINKING
ABOUT YOU DEAR
NOW YOU ARE
SO FAR AWAY,
HERE IN THE HOME
WHERE YOU'VE
LAUGHED & TALKED
WE SIT AND WE HOPE AND PRAY.

WE ASK THAT YOUR HEALTH AND
YOUR STRENGTH MAY BE
AS BONNIE & GOOD AS OF YORE
AND LONG FOR THE DAY WHEN YOU HOMEWARD COME,
AND YOUR DEAR STEP SOUNDS AT THE DOOR.

6.   580.G.   COPYRIGHT   BEAGLES POSTCARDS

7. Early in 1915 The Cairo Postcard Trust was established in Cairo by some enterprising British businessmen who realised that there was a fortune to be made by selling cards to the tens of thousands of soldiers who were crowded into Cairo. The Trust's cards were pleasantly designed and generally evoked images of home. The writer of this one was R.H.E., on 17 December 1917. *Too late to send Christmas card so send this instead. Let you know I haven't forgot you. Dick done much hunting this season, I often think of him. Ton's of love to you three. XXX.* R.H.E. was evidently writing to his family but the envelope in which he sent the card no longer exists.

7.

8. This card is of French design, as shown by the military uniforms and the 75mm gun – used only by the French – as well as the girl's curls and her mock-military cap. However, the verse was printed in English only and it was posted in England on 30 October 1916 to Miss Suzanne Alloucherie in Lillers, France. *My dear Suzanne, Very many thanks for your welcome card received last week, glad you are all well as we are in good health. Our boys are still safe but find it cold, the weather is awful wet. Did you get my letter and newspaper I sent over 3 weeks ago. Also the little table cloth that Mother and Dad sent to Mrs. Alloucherie. Fondest love to all, Yours ever Cissie XXXXX.*

The War in Rhyme

9. Raphael Tuck's cards were usually more graphic than this one, which shows two seamen ashore with a Gattling gun. Naval shore parties did use Gattlings during river campaigns in the further reaches of Empire but the pose here is unrealistic. However, it links the gun crew with the notion of running the enemy ashore, as expressed in a verse from 'Hearts of Oak'.

To arms, to arms, ye brave!
The avenging sword unsheath:
March on, march on!
All hearts resolved on liberty or death.

8.

We ne'er see our foes but
   we wish them to stay,
They never see us but they
   wish us away.
If they run, why we follow,
   and run them ashore
And if they won't fight us
   we cannot do more.
   "Hearts of Oak."

9.

10. An artist's attempt to illustrate the greatest British marching song of the war. The preliminary verse was rarely sung but the chorus was shouted, hummed and whistled ad nauseum. A.

Pearse shows an elderly Flemishwoman giving wine to passing soldiers outside her home, which looks much more like an English cottage than a Flemish one.

"IT'S A LONG, LONG WAY FROM TIPPERARY."

10.

A REFRESHER—ON THE WAY TO YPRES.

Up to mighty London came an Irishman one day,
As the streets are paved with gold, sure ev'ryone was gay,
Singing songs of Piccadilly, Strand and Leicester Square,
Till Paddy got excited, then he shouted to them there :—
"It's a long way to Tipperary, it's a long way to go;
It's a long way to Tipperary, to the sweetest girl I know !
Good-bye Piccadilly, farewell Leicester Square,
It's a long long way to Tipperary, but my heart's right there !"
By permission B. Feldman & Co., 2 & 3 Arthur St., London, W.C

134

The War in Rhyme

11. This card, from Bamforth's 'Hymn' series, is flowery enough to have been of French design. It is extremely rare to find a guardian angel on a British postcard. The banners carried by the soldiers forming up for battle bear St George's Cross and are pure poetic licence. British troops carried no banners in battle during the Great War, except on one occasion during the Battle of Neuve Chapelle in 1915. The young officer, praying before joining his men, has a cap rather than a steel helmet but the card is of 1918 rather than 1914/15, as might be expected from the cap. The reverse has a single sentence: *To Maud with best love from Sandy.*

12 – 14. These three cards, relating to Australia, include a rare example of signed verse rich in imagery. The very first line establishes the homeland with the word homestead. Note the spelling of revally; since the correct spelling of reveille has almost the same pronunciation as the mis-spelt word it is possible that neither poet nor printer realised it was an error. Or perhaps the poet used what he imagined to be a soldier's spelling. The vast distance between the soldier and his loved ones, 12,000 miles between the Western Front and Sydney, was a frequent theme on Australian postcards.

The multiple image of 'Hands Across the Sea' does not actually show Australia but it was sent by an Australian soldier to his mother, Mrs L.S. Ritchie, 76 Windsor St.,

Paddington, Sydney. *At Sea, March 1918. My Dear Mother. Not having very much news to give you I thought I'd drop you this card and let you see I'm safe and well. Wrote Mrs. Turner yesterday and Miss Gale. Had a concert on board was very good indeed. Got a good job on board this boat, will have tons of splosh* [money] *when I arrive. Love to all at home. Your son, Harold R.*

By the time he sent his card 'Good Luck to a Sister at Home', Private Ritchie was on active service in France with a company of the 4th Battalion A.I.F. The date was 26 April 1918. *To Dear Willie with very best love & Good Wishes from your Brother.* Pte Ritchie transferred to the 35th Battalion and returned home in 1919.

The Boys

Ah, 'tis lonesome in the homestead
While the lads are far away;
And the hearts they've left behind them
Can but quietly wait and pray,
Keeping still the old lamp burning
And the latch loose on the door,
For the welcome ones returning
When the weary war is o'er.

And the lads themselves are thinking
Of the faces ever dear;
And Remembrance, in the darkness,
Brings the loved ones very near;
And the dismal hour of vigil
Loses more than half its pain,
For the thought, like prayer, within it,
Of the coming home again.

There are many softly sleeping,
Who shall never more awake
Till God's sudden trumpet sounding
Shall upon their slumber break;
But they'll leap to that revally,
Ever faithful, brave, and true,
And we'll see them stepping proudly
In God's final great review.

So in stillness of the evening,
Or when stirs the call of day,
To our God in highest heaven
May our spirits ever pray,—
That He'll bring our boys back to us,
When the time of pain is o'er,
Or lead us, where they shall wait us,
Clothed in victory, evermore.
Lauchlan MacLean Watt.

HANDS ACROSS THE SEA

Tho' the ocean rolls between
Friendship holds us fast,
And aye, while life itself shall run,
So shall our friendship last.

13.

Good Luck.

**To a SISTER at Home.
From a BROTHER on the Roam.**

A Soldier's Verse-Letter.

Dear Sister, if you had been born a boy,
You'd be acting a Soldier's part;
And would brave it well, through thick
    and thin,
With courage and right good heart.

But being a girl, darling Sister,
And remaining at Dear Old Home;
You must know that you're never
    forgotten,
By a Brother who's on the roam.

For he thinks of his Sister daily,
And pictures her day's work through;
While he knows that she's doing some-
    thing
To help Old England, too!

So these lines, Sis, accept as a letter,
For we haven't much leisure here;
They are simply to send Fondest
    Greetings.
To a SISTER I hold most dear.

V. S., copyright.

14.

15 – 17. The story of 'The Pardon Came Too Late' did not merely pluck at the heartstrings of the time, it wrenched them, using both words and images. The verse is woeful and the poses and presentation are unrealistic – the executed soldier shows no signs of having been hit by the firing squad's bullets. However, the series does underline the fate which might await a soldier found guilty of desertion, especially if he had deserted under fire. Courts martial of 1914–18 were not noted for their leniency and some generals, who were in a position to commute a sentence, were pitiless. A total of 318 British soldiers were shot by firing squad between 1914 and 1920.

THE PARDON CAME TOO LATE (1).

A fair-haired boy in a foreign land, at sunrise was to die;
In a prison cell he sat alone, from his heart there came a sigh;
Deserted from the ranks they said, the reason none could say,
They only know the orders were that he should die next day.
And as the hours glided by, a messenger on wings did fly,
To save this boy from such a fate, a pardon, but it came too late.

15.   BAMFORTH (COPYRIGHT).

The War in Rhyme

16.

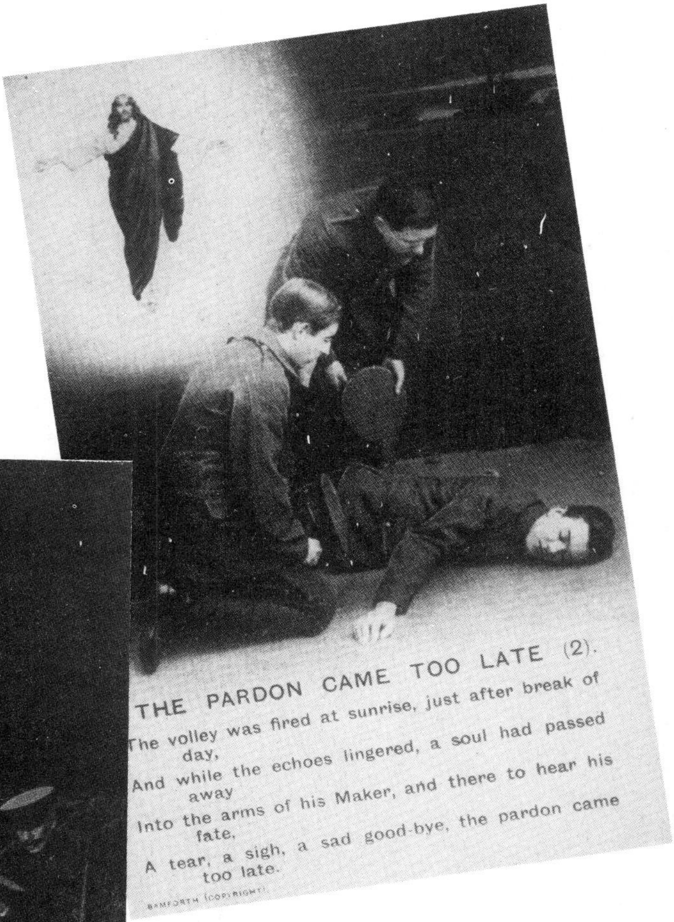

THE PARDON CAME TOO LATE (2).

The volley was fired at sunrise, just after break of
 day,
And while the echoes lingered, a soul had passed
 away
Into the arms of his Maker, and there to hear his
 fate,
A tear, a sigh, a sad good-bye, the pardon came
 too late.

BAMFORTH (COPYRIGHT)

THE PARDON CAME TOO LATE (3).

And 'round the camp fire burning bright, the story then was
 told
How his mother on a dying bed called for her son so bold;
He hastened to obey her wish, was captured on the way;
She never saw her boy, so fair, he died at break of day,
And when the truth at last was known, his innocence at once
 was shown,
To save from such an unjust fate, a pardon sent, but 'twas
 too late.

AMFORTH (COPYRIGHT)

17.

139

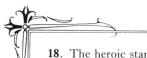

18. The heroic stanza of this card was accompanied by the classic patriotic symbol of flags and standards. Together, verse and symbols were a direct appeal to patriotism and published for the more 'educated market' than for soldiers. The card was sent to Miss Ethel Milne, Erin Port, Liscard, Cheshire.

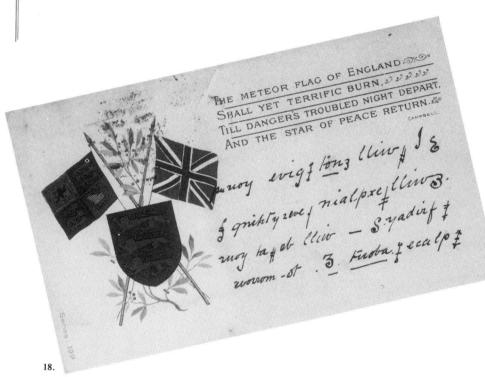

18.

The War in Rhyme

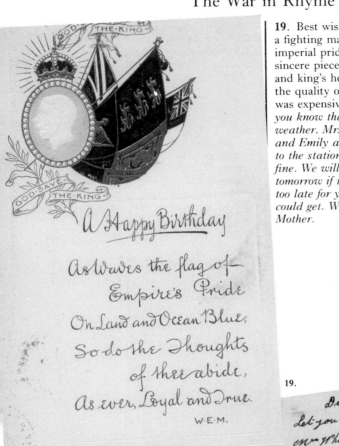

A Happy Birthday

As Waves the flag of
Empire's Pride
On Land and Ocean Blue,
So do the Thoughts
of thee abide,
As ever, Loyal and True.

W·E·M·

19. Best wishes for a happy birthday to a fighting man are linked here with imperial pride and a rather trite but sincere piece of verse. The flags, crown and king's head are embossed to add to the quality of the card which, at 2*d.*, was expensive in 1917. *Just a line to let you know that we are having lovely weather. Mrs. Whallis arrived today and Emily and I went swanking down to the station in the motor car. It was fine. We will be going to Morpeth tomorrow if it is fine. The card is a little too late for your birthday but it is all I could get. With love from Emily and Mother.*

20. The verse on this postcard is unusually interesting. In translation, it reads:

Our Frontier

Our Virtuous Maiden
Do you know the frontier,
  Our frontier?
It's made of heather,
  The frontier,
Of marjoram and holly,
  Our frontier.

It was so beautiful,
  Our frontier,
That the jealous-hearted
Germans wanted it entirely,
  Our frontier.

They crossed the frontier,
  Our frontier,
Keeping it a prisoner,
Made it moan under the blows,
  Our frontier.

It is not dead, the frontier,
  Our frontier,
It still hopes to see beautiful days,
  Our frontier.
In spite of you our frontier
Will come back to us.

It will join again the other frontier,
  Our frontier,
A short time ago bordered by
  the Rhine,
Rocked by its eddies,
  Our frontier.

And it's there that
  Our frontier is
Waiting for us in the heather,
  Our frontier,
Marjoram and holly,
  Our frontier.

The postcard was sent on 21 September 1915 to a soldier of the 364th Regiment on the Portal Sector of the Western Front. *Dear cousin, We send you our greetings from Alfortville. Everything is all right at home and we hope the same applies to you. We both embrace you. Maria and Hubert Quemand.*

LA FRONTIÈRE DE CHEZ NOUS
par Léon Michel
Air : *La Rosière de chez nous*

Connaissez-vous la frontière,
La frontière de chez nous?
Elle est faite de bruyère,
  La frontière, (bis)
De marjolaine et de houx,
La frontière de chez nous.

Si belle était la frontière,
La frontière de chez nous,
Que la voulaient tout entière,
  La frontière, (bis)
Les Germains au cœur jaloux,
La frontière de chez nous.

Ils ont franchi la frontière,
La frontière de chez nous,
Et la gardant prisonnière,
  La frontière, (bis)
L'ont fait gémir sous les coups,
La frontière de chez nous.

N'est pas morte la frontière,
La frontière de chez nous.
En de beaux jours elle espère,
  La frontière, (bis)
Nous reviendra malgré vous,
La frontière de chez nous.

Rejoindra l'autre frontière,
La frontière de chez nous,
Que le Rhin bordait naguère,
  La frontière. (bis)
La berçant de ses remous,
La frontière de chez nous.

Et c'est là que la frontière,
La frontière de chez nous,
Nous attend dans la bruyère,
  La frontière, (bis)
La marjolaine et le houx,
La frontière de chez nous.

Extrait du *Bulletin des
Années de la République.*

20.

142

CHAPTER THIRTEEN

Entente Cordiale

The term 'Entente Cordiale' was much used in parliament, press and propaganda from 1914 to 1917. Britain and France had formed the alliance in 1904, but it was only a settlement of imperial differences, not a treaty with obligations to help each other in time of war.

Britain backed the French acquisition of Morocco in return for French recognition of Britain's rights in Egypt. When Germany tried to bully France over Morocco the Entente was strengthened. Foreign observers thought than an entente between Britain and France was bizarre; after all, they had fought against each other in one war after another for centuries.

That the Entente not only survived but gained strength was due to a lessening of tension between the two great nations as they now no longer coveted each other's imperial possessions. The British and French found that they had much in common in the face of the newly imperialist, upstart Germans.

Under a treaty of 1839, Britain was a guarantor of Belgium's neutrality and went to war against Germany when that country invaded Belgium, on 4 August 1914, as a prelude to invading France. Britain was not bound by treaty to help France – or Russia, another target for Germany – but the British Foreign Secretary, Earl Grey, and part of the government considered it imperative that Britain should go to war on the side of France and Russia. He reasoned that if either one or both were defeated there would be little to prevent Germany from overwhelming the British Empire.

Throughout the Great War political and military relations between the British and French were often uneasy. Army commanders from both nations were disinclined to take orders from the other and General French, commanding the British Expeditionary Force, 1914–15, sometimes foolishly refused to discuss strategy and tactics with his French counterpart. However, the German army was too big and powerful for either France or Britain to face alone so great efforts were made to maintain cordial relations – the *cordiale* of the entente.

Each nation's leaders praised the military prowess of the other and handed out decorations to each

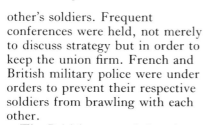

other's soldiers. Frequent conferences were held, not merely to discuss strategy but in order to keep the union firm. French and British military police were under orders to prevent their respective soldiers from brawling with each other.

The British assumed that the Entente would hold firm and any propaganda to strengthen and maintain it was muted. Indeed, no British postcard publisher was interested in cards about the Entente; they just did not look like becoming big sellers. The French, on the other hand, flooded the market with Entente cards. They were encouraged by the French ministries of information and propaganda. Cards of this type were popular in the war zone with both British and French soldiers, though more so with the French. This may have been because the captions were generally in French. From the marketing viewpoint, bilingual texts would have made more sense.

In the popular British view Belgium became part of the Entente when it was invaded by Germany, as did any country which fought the Germans, such as Serbia and Russia. On some postcards Japan is shown as a member of the Entente, although that country's participation in the war was limited to providing naval escorts for Allied troopships. The French seemed to draw great comfort from having their allies around them, hence the tacit extension of the Entente to include all Germany's enemies.

Entente Cordiale

1. The classic Entente Cordiale brothers-in-arms, the Poilu and the Tommy. It would be interesting to know why, in this 1915 picture, the photographer posed the French soldier bayonet fixed to his Lebel while the English soldier still has his in its scabbard. The message on the reverse reads: *5th Batt., Cheshire Regiment. Dear Miss Thanks very much for the parcel you sent me it came in very handy to take to the trenches Harry Cadman has got wounded in the shoulder on April 15th while we were digging a small trench to drain the water out of the firing trench. No more now at present I remain Yours sincerely Percy.*

2. These two figures appear in many postcards – the classic Woman of France with her friend The English Officer – a second lieutenant in fact. The card was written in French on 29 March 1915, by Louise Heughebaert to 'My dear little George'. She arranges to meet him from a train and she will see him soon – with love.

1.

2.

3. The two models are following the French photographer's instructions to the letter. The supposed Scottish soldier has been bloodlessly wounded near the heart. He has been told to look stricken unto death and his face has been retouched in a pallid tone on the master photograph to emphasise his serious condition. His French comrade, while supporting him, glares his defiance at the common enemy and will use his Lebel rifle one-handed to defend him if necessary. The Scot is wearing a remarkable uniform, not one ever seen by a genuine Scottish soldier. His sporran is astonishing and, on examination, is based on a woman's wig. It is then buttoned to his waistbelt, instead of being suspended around the waist with straps or chain. The make-up of his legwear is a matter for speculation. Among British troops cards such as this caused great amusement.

4. The publishers considered, correctly, that no caption was needed for this human scene, as a British soldier shows a French comrade a photograph of his family. It was unlabelled Entente Cordiale. The enigmatic message, written in Flemish, says: *So if you go up to your door you'll have to put on your police hat. The blessing of Mummy and Daddy.*

3.   146   4.

Entente Cordiale

5. Here the Entente Cordiale is linked to the defence of French womanhood. No matter how they posed their models, the French photographers never seemed able to make them take their work seriously. Equally, they had great difficulty, apparently, in acquiring authentic uniforms. The British uniform used here is ludicrous. The card was sent to Madame Veuve, for a happy birthday, with prosperity and good health.

6. All for one and one for all, this 1915 card proclaims. 'All' were, from the left, a Russian soldier, a Frenchman, a Belgian or Serbian and a British warrior, who wears the strangest unmilitary footwear. The card is most interesting for the early bi-plane which can be seen aloft.

Le Progrès et la Civilisation sont à l'ombre de nos couleurs   23

5.

Tous pour Un Un pour Tous

6.

7. Another awkwardly posed group of Allies – a Belgian, then two Tommies and two poilus. On the reverse, in French, is *Affectionate kisses, see you soon, Eline.*

8. Again, the Allies show their defiance with a rhyming couplet which, translated, reads:

'By sea, land or air if danger comes
We aren't afraid of the Prussian rage.'

The uniform provided for the make-believe Tommy did not fit him – note the overlong sleeve – and his fancy boots would not have lasted two miles marching on French cobbles. The message, in French, is brief: *Hullo from Blendecques* (a Flemish town). The designer has used the same aircraft as on p. 148 but now its nose gunner has shot down an enemy plane.

7.

8.

Entente Cordiale

LES ALLIÉS DANS LA TRANCHÉE.
·importe plus ou moins d'atout,
est l'allemand qui prendra tout.

Revanche
159

9. 'The Allies in the Trench', proclaims the legend of this card. The rhyming couplet: 'It's of no importance to have more or fewer trumps; It's the Germans who will take everything.' The message on the reverse, in French, is dated 18 July 1915. *Dear Uncle: May the postcard bring us victory, good health and happiness to see our beloved people back. From this day, Sunday, I thought I would have received a letter from you or auntie. Hoping to receive a letter from you. Kindest regards. Marcel* By their scores of thousands, soldiers wrote to request or implore a letter. Entente Cordiale, so strong in the dugout, has not reached the battlefield (above), where only French soldiers are present.

10. Leaders of the Allied nations frequently appeared on postcards, especially in combination to show that 'unity creates strength' – to liberally translate the French. Many French people were embarrassed that they had no monarch to join George, Albert and Nicolas, just a president, Poincare. While this card highlights 1914, in small figures underneath are 1915 and 1916.

HONNEUR PATRIE
POINCARE PRESIDENT DE LA REPUBLIQUE
S.M. NICOLAS II EMPEREUR DE RUSSIE
1914
L'UNION FAIT LA FORCE
GEORGES V ROI D'ANGLETERRE
S.M. ALBERT I.er ROI DES BELGES

10.

World War I in Postcards

11. An Entente Cordiale of a different kind, produced by Biscuits 'Olibet', the 'Premiere Marque Française' – the leading French brand. This card was one of a 'Collection de Guerre' of 1915. The artist plays tricks with faces and uniforms. Having written 'Frenchmen always like the Japanese', he puts a French uniform on a Japanese and a Scottish uniform on the Frenchman. Even then, the Frenchman's visage is somewhat Oriental. The spoon in the sock, rather than the traditional skean dhu dagger, was the artist's final fun. The Japanese came into the war on the Allied side but only to provide naval escorts for Allied troopships.

11. *Les français ont toujours aimé le japon*

150

Entente Cordiale

12. Emphasis on the spirit of unity among the Allies was occasionally supplied by postcards such as this one, from a painting by the Belgian artist Maurice Wagemans. Showing a British soldier raising his hat in salute to Belgian, French, British and Russian wounded, the card was published by Raphael Tuck and all profits were given to the Wounded Allies Relief Committee.

12.

TUCK'S POST CARD

CARTE POSTALE.

By Appointment

"The Allies."

The original of this remarkable artistic picture, of which this Photogravure Postcard is a faithful reproduction, is executed in Pastel by the famous Belgian artist, Maurice Wagemans. It is now in the possession of the Rt. Hon. Lord Swaythling. The proceeds of the sale of both the original and the postcards are devoted entirely to the invaluable work of the Wounded Allies Relief Committee.

(For Address Only.)

Raphael Tuck & Sons' "Photogravure" Postcard.
ART PUBLISHERS TO THEIR MAJESTIES THE KING & QUEEN

Printed in England.

13. This card, one of Tuck's 'Oilette' range, was, in effect dedicated to the Allies, with the flags of the Allied nations assembled around the winged figure of Victory. Tuck's were always hyperconscious of their royal connection – 'Art Publishers by Appointment to Their Majesties the King and Queen'. The reverse carries an extract from a speech by the Prime Minister, David Lloyd George, on 4 August 1917. 'This is the third anniversary of the greatest war the world has ever witnessed. What are we fighting for? To defeat the most dangerous conspiracy ever plotted against the liberty of nations, carefully, skilfully, insidiously, clandestinely planned in every detail with ruthless, cynical determination.'

13.

CHAPTER FOURTEEN

Our Brave Allies – the French

The contrast between French and British postcards of the Great War continues to intrigue me even after a lifetime spent studying the two races at war. Sometimes I shake my head in disbelief when I look at a French design, since my more conservative British soul cannot readily accept what appears to be grotesque bad taste. Almost every idea – and French card designers were fertile in ideas – seems to be overdone.

British designers and producers did not employ actors, dressed as soldiers, to model for postcard photographers. The French did this constantly, often in ill-fitting, inaccurate uniforms. With rare exceptions, these male models never managed to look like real soldiers. When they were not wooden they were self-conscious in front of the camera so that all illusion was lost. The same models turn up with the same props on dozens of cards and it is likely that a photographer took all the photographs on one day.

Colourful flowers abound, even sprouting from the muzzles of rifles and nestling in soldiers' arms. The martial image does not generally accommodate flowers – certainly not in British, American and German cards. In any case, most of the flowers used by the French postcard makers were made of paper and given bright, unnatural colours.

In French cards photographs predominate over drawings and there is the inescapable impression that the photographers were enthusiastic amateurs. They rarely succeeded in relaxing their subjects, who look embarrassingly camera-conscious, and they outrageously overdid the props.

There is no mistaking the values which the French held most dear – honour and the flag, readiness to die for France, the vision of glory, the virtue of women, defiance, strength and courage. Unlike the British, the French produced special war theme cards for Easter and New Year. The British had Christmas postcards but generally they were of regimental origin.

Women, usually glorified and romanticised, appear on many

French postcards, often in what was supposed to be classical Grecian costume. They are also frequently dressed as nurse-nuns giving succour and comfort to wounded or dying soldiers. In other cards they exemplified, apparently, all that the French soldiers considered worth dying for. Women were supposed to inspire the French warriors and the poilus' taste for cards of this nature indicates that the supposition may have been correct, even though, to the foreign eye, the women are unreal.

However, I have never seen a French postcard of the war which in any way reduces the dignity of women. French women are rarely shown flirting with French soldiers, though a few designs show them doing this with British soldiers.

As French postcards were much more generally available in France than British cards they were bought in large numbers by British soldiers in estaminets, stationery and gift shops. In this way, hundreds of thousands of them were sent back to Blighty and to the Dominions. The great majority have disappeared, but those which do remain provide a vivid picture of French attitudes, values and tastes between the years 1914 and 1919.

Our Brave Allies – the French

1. The idealised French woman of the war, complete with heavenly trumpet, angel's wings, national flag and Grecian sandals. The dedication to 'Honour and the flag', was a recurring theme.

2. A typical French New Year card. The model is properly attired but his puttees are incorrectly rolled around his legs and his stance is that of a model, not of a soldier. As for the flowers stuck in his rifle . . . ! The anonymous writer, addressing Mademoiselle Leontine Durand, wishes her a good and happy new year of 1918.

1.

2.

3. It is difficult to believe that this fresh-faced, clean-shaven young man in his mock-heroic pose is a real soldier, 'on the front'. In characteristically aggressive verse, the Boche is told that the French are coming to settle their old debt, which will be discharged 'on the bayonet'. The writer thanks his dear Lucie for the cards she has been sending him. The weather has been good but winter is approaching. It is, in fact, 10 October 1918. He asks Lucie to embrace his mother for him, always a diplomatic request from a soldier to a girl.

4. The French were fond of cards showing wounded soldiers being tended by nurses. Without distinction, we are told here, the sister devotedly cares for the wounded (blesses). Writing to Mademoiselle Leontine Durand, her soldier correspondent says: *The war does not make one forget ones friends. On the contrary, this is why I am sending you best wishes for your birthday.*

3.

4.

Our Brave Allies – the French

5. It is hard to imagine any pose more atificial than that of the nursing sister on this card. The flags in the background, including the British flag, have been brought into the studio from the props room. Loosely translated the caption reads: 'Life in the field hospital sometimes has great attractions after one has given up the profession of arms.'

6. Another male model is coaxed to look adoringly at 'the angels of pain'. The caption reads: 'Your smile is a powerful balm, which makes a convalescent of a wounded soldier.'

L'ANGE DE LA DOULEUR!

PATRIOTIC 1269

Votre sourire est un baume puissant
Qui d'un blessé, fait un convalescent!

6.

La vie a l'ambulance a parfois de grands charmes
L'on y renoncerait au dur métier des armes

5.

7. Yet another fabricated hospital scene, showing a 'good sister' tending a wounded man. The bottles on the bedside table look suspiciously like cognac and wine.

8. This interesting card, of October 1914, clearly shows the absurd uniform worn by French troops early in the war. The blue jacket and the red pantaloons were easy targets for enemy soldiers. 'His weapon is not dead in your hands', says the legend. The gallant nurse steps across the dead warrior to take his place in the battle, her clenched fist showing her determination. The rifle is the Lebel, the standard French personal firearm of the war. The card was sent from one girl, Marie, to another, Leontine. *I hope that your little beetle is always good. I am well too. Thank you for your letter. I wish you courage. A thousand kisses from your cousin.* The allusion to the 'little beetle' is one of many which, decades later, can only remain mystifying.

9. Dated 16 July 1915, this postcard shows a nurse, complete with first-aid kit, tending a badly wounded soldier on the battlefield. That the sender of the card was deeply moved by the drawing and its accompanying verse is shown by the way he has written 'France for ever' on the front of the card. Translated here as prose, the verse reads: 'To dress with her fine soft fingers wounded men lying motionless in the naked countryside. Divine pity descended among us. She was about to fly away as she had come when the little soldier, humble cannon fodder, wanted to know at least the name of the unknown woman. And the goddess, in order to leave her name, took a beautiful white

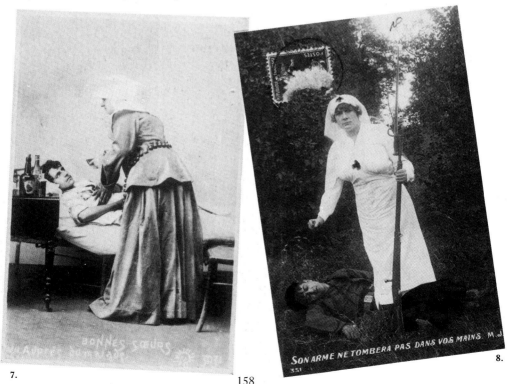

7.

8.

SON ARME NE TOMBERA PAS DANS VOS MAINS. M.J

Our Brave Allies – the French

piece of cloth and with a smile, having dipped her finger in the blood of the wounded, she drew a cross, not knowing what to write. And the women of France have put it on their arm.' Here again the nurse symbolises French womanhood. The story, as told in verse, is a lovely one, but it is fantasy. The number of women, nurses or others, who reached the actual battlefield could be counted on the fingers of one man's hands. The sender of the postcard, Emile, has managed, in his fine hand, to crowd much information onto the card for his friend Jules. Translated from the French: *Thanks for the letter. Hullo to old friends. In this countryside it's very hot. I'm already used to the messtin. A few words to tell you I have been at Sarlet since Monday noon. I haven't had the time to write before departure. Anyhow, your mother will have told you that I made the journey with a priest, the Abbe Pels. We were only two to arrive that day. They appointed Pels without rank to the major's H.Q. office. I have met many people from Dunkirk. The 14th July [Bastille Day] was a real day of festivity as you can see by the menu: Soup, roast, saute potatoes, peas, cheese, coffee and liqueur. As much wine as we wished. One thing bothers me – it's being so far away from home. Finally, I am waiting for the pleasure to see you. A cordial handshake.* Elsewhere on the card, Emile notes that he looked for a Marius Vauelle but could not find him. The R. DEVOS stamped on the card is the name of the censor.

9.

10. Even in the midst of war the French did not forget their religious occasions. This card, for Happy Easter, was sent by Benois Maurice, of 28th Company, 63rd Infantry Regiment, to Monsieur Albert and his family. *A souvenir from a soldier of the class of 1915 who embraces you.*

11. No British postcard publisher would have risked his money on this card. 'Graine de Poilu' – Soldier's Seed – straight from birth is armed and, in the ranks of the 15th Infantry Regiment, ready to deal with the Boche. It was brought out by Edition Patriotique for 'Guerre Europeenne 1914–16'. The dates may indicate that the publishers believed the conflict would not go on into 1917.

10.

Y en a-t-il encore des Boches ?
Are there some more Germans ?
Есть ли еще проклятые нѣмцы ?

11.

Our Brave Allies – the French

12. This design shows the ever-present symbolism of defending the children of France. The poilu draws his sword to protect 'the little girl he adores with all his heart'. The card certainly appealed to an English soldier, who wrote on the back, *To Jackie from Daddy France 1917*.

13. One of several postcard visions of war. 'The Republic calls us, to conquer or die'. The presence of the German soldier on the right, identifiable from his pickelhaube headdress and his pack, is puzzling.

12.

13.

14. An interesting, if artificial, card of 1915 showing, left, a French chasseur and, right, an Italian chasseur. Chasseurs – literally, hunters – were the equivalent of the British light infantry. The two countries will always be allies, according to the legend. On the reverse a soldier named Nestor, writing to dear Suzanne, says that the courage of the soldiers and their faith in God, will preserve them and see them through to victory.

14.

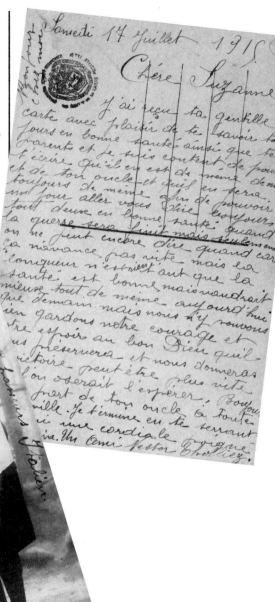

162

Our Brave Allies – the French

15. Again, the soldier with his flowers, and against an unmilitary background. The pose of the right leg betokens the model; it is not a stance one would associate with the military bearing of a soldier. This card is without any slogan or message.

16. This postcard is stuffed with French idealism. The little girl, holding her flag, gestures her defiance. The angel of victory, brandishing the Allied flags, hovers over the field while French cocks chase off the German eagle. In the left background is the stairway to eventual peace. *Little father, I want to tell you that we are not afraid for your wellbeing.*

15.

16.

17. Modern Frenchmen who see this card are embarrassed by its clumsy sentiment. The designers have the Eternal French Woman saying: 'Soldiers march on, plant our magic flag in Berlin and cry "Long live the Republic!"' The sender of the card does not comment on it, perhaps because he is excited about getting leave to see his family. He then writes, as a postscript, *I have obtained 30 days extra.*

18. The sender of this card dates it 6 July 1918. By this time the war had been going on for nearly four years and the daybreak of glory (Aurore de Gloire) must have seemed a long way off. The blue-clad poilu model was told to reflect on the carnage of the war, shown in the foreground, but to see the sun of hope rising behind it. The message, from a cavalryman, reads: *Dear friends. Forgive me for not having written earlier but we have had many changes. I think that my brother or my little nieces will have talked to you about it. I am back at the front for a month. I have changed regiments. I found the regiment at rest and I'm taking advantage of this and am happy and well fed. I don't know if we will be* *able to stay here for long. No other news. Nearly time for the holidays.* [August was the traditional French holiday month.] *Oh, you lucky things. For me it's six months. So I'm leaving you with kind regards.*

Soldats allez planter notre Drapeau magique À Berlin en criant : Vive la République!

17.

Aurore de Gloire

18.

Our Brave Allies – the French

19. This New Year card, showing a girl in provincial dress, possibly of the Loire region, brought with it, in 1916, the best wishes of Jeanne, Blanche, Lorence, Audine and Marie. Lucky soldier to have five belles behind the lines!

20. Flowers displayed with the soldier's helmet are oddly incongruous, but this is actually a New Year card for 1916. The secondary image is that of the violent war continuing. French postcard artists generally improved on Nature's colours for flowers, as can be seen here.

19.

20.

21. A postcard drawing of 1914 invokes an image of Napoleon fighting a battle in the same place, Montmirail, a century before. Napoleon appears in several French designs, partly because he represented victory but also because he symbolised French nationalism. Napoleon defeated the Prussian Marshal Blucher, on 11 February 1814, and in three other batles, all within five days. In those four battles the French suffered a total of 2,000 casualties. In 1914 they lost 20,000 men in one battle.

22. The conscript of 1915 and the veteran, who wears the Medaille Militaire and the Legion d'Honneur. 'Ah', he says, 'If I could have another twenty years I would depart content.' The theme of an old soldier encouraging or inspiring a recruit was a durable one. In the background is Les Invalides, the great home in Paris for old soldiers.

21.

22.

Our Brave Allies – the French

AU MUSÉE DE L'ARMÉE

Les 9 Drapeaux pris à l'ennemi jusqu'au 1er Janvier 1915

23.

23. The capture of enemy standards meant little to the British Army in the First World War but to the French they were a source of great pride. This was a throwback to earlier times when the taking of a regimental flag could mean, in effect, the destruction of the enemy unit. It would then have no rallying point and its morale could collapse. These were the German flags, nine of them, captured up to 1 January 1915.

24. This was a risque and decidedly suggestive card in 1917. A soldier at the front receives a letter telling him of the birth of a child – the result of 'a lovely thrust of the bayonet'. The infant is now seven days old. On the reverse a soldier with an indecipherable signature has written to Madame E. Laveau of Rueil, in the Seine and Oise province. Translated from the French, *Take notice! I will be a godfather. Excuse the liberty – I embrace you affectionately.*

DES 7 JOURS

SOUVENIR

Un beau coup de baïonnette !

24.

25. This is how the French saw the British and Indian soldiers, ready not only with rifle and bayonet but flag held weapon-like as well. The Indian figure and the bell tents in the background appear in several similar postcards. The card, dated 5 July 1915, reads: *Sonnie, Thanks very much for sweets you sent. Uncle will send something home for you some day.*

26. A poilu in a freshly laundered uniform is superimposed on a trench scene while he makes a proud, defiant threat – 'We will drive out the Boche!' The card was sent from the Yser River front, on the extreme northern edge of the Western Front, on 19 April 1918. The writer, a French soldier who does not sign his name, tells his family and friends that the weather is very cold and that he is living in snow. In spite of *the fire of the struggle* he is still in good health and he hopes that the card finds them in the same happy state. However, he complains about lack of news from home. *Once again the letters do not reach us* . . . . French soldiers claimed, with justification, that their postal service was not as efficient as that of their British comrades.

Ever Ready

25.

Nous les bouterons dehors ces Boches!

26.

Our Brave Allies – the French

27. Entitled 'Respects of France to Military Valour', this card shows the principal French decorations. From the left, the Medaille Militaire, established in 1852; the Legion d'Honneur, instituted in 1802, and the premier French military decoration; the Croix de Guerre, in this case with a silver star signifying a Divisional Mention in Despatches. The card, the last of four, was sent to Mrs A. Bryant, 9 Lysander Gardens, Upper Holloway, London. It begins in the middle of a sentence which had started on card number three . . . . *only that it was a bit stale being so long in coming. You must think no wonder for packing it so well. I can tell you I am looking for a letter from you. Trusting you are keeping well and do not worry so cheer up my dear. Well fondest love and kisses to my darling from yours Arthur.*

28. This card carries an eloquent exhortation to the nation as a whole and soldiers in particular. 'French people, look what you defend!' Within the outline of France is all that the French soldier held most dear – wife and child, beloved, aged parents, his religion and his homeland, illustrated by the tree and haystack.

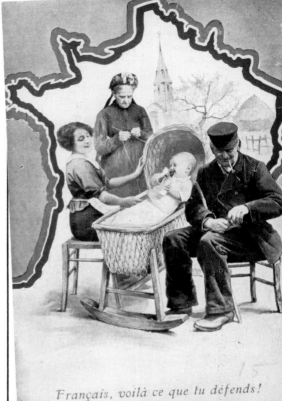

Français, voilà ce que tu défends!

28.

Suprême Recompense

Hommages de la France à la Valeur Militaire.

27.

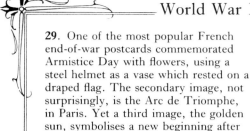

29. One of the most popular French end-of-war postcards commemorated Armistice Day with flowers, using a steel helmet as a vase which rested on a draped flag. The secondary image, not surprisingly, is the Arc de Triomphe, in Paris. Yet a third image, the golden sun, symbolises a new beginning after the clouds of war.

30. A French Alpine soldier in his distinctive uniform rests on a studio log adorned with the paper flowers which so appealed to the French. Though separated by war and long distance, soldier and sweetheart both display the same flower. The rhyming couplet is put into the girl's mouth. 'These flowers have grown on high summits. I believe you are sincere and I submit.' The message on the back of the card, in Flemish, was written on 10 October 1918, to Miss Julia. *It was a pleasure to receive your card, seeing that you are in good health, as I am for the time being. Miss Julia, this is the time the beetroots start smiling at you but from now on they will be cold. I resemble beetroots. At night I am always cold too. Do me a little favour. If you care to sleep with me I think I would not be so cold, for such young girls are always in great heat. So, let me end my card with a handshake from far away. Accept my best wishes, your friend Jules Noyer.* On the side of the card Jules added: *Many greetings to the whole household.* The card was sent in an envelope so that Julia would not be embarrassed. Nobody of the household need have known of Jules' wish to sleep with her. He was, after all, merely expressing a fantasy wish felt by millions of soldiers.

29.

30.

Our Brave Allies – the French

31. More posed flirtation between soldier and sweetheart. The legend is 'The Aims of War'. The rhyming couplet is in the form of question and answer. 'What does one put in the peace treaty? The mutual clause of the most favoured passion.' The 'favourite passion', is, of course, love. On the reverse, Gervais, on 24 March 1918, writes to Miss Louise. *On my way to join the mates – a sad thing. Greetings to your mother. Receive this with my best love.*

32. This card could well be classified as an Entente Cordiale or Brave Allies type but it was intended purely for French consumption and wholly for propaganda purposes. All France's allies are shown 'saluting the soldiers of Verdun'. Their courage in this inferno deserved salute. The card quotes in full General Joffre's Order of the Day,

which was intended to encourage the fighting men. This is the essence of the order: 'For three weeks you have been undergoing a formidable assault by the enemy. Germany has anticipated the success of her efforts, which she believed to be irresistible, and for a while she concentrated her best troops and strongest artillery. She had hoped that the taking of Verdun would strengthen the courage of her allies and convince neutral countries of German superiority. She had not taken *you* into consideration. Night and day, in spite of an unprecedented bombardment, you have resisted all attacks and have maintained your positions. The struggle isn't over yet, for the Germans need a victory. You could wrench victory from him. We have an abundance of ammunition and many reserves but above all you have an indomitable courage and your faith in the destiny of the Republic. The country watches you. You will be among those of whom people will say "They are barring the Germans from the road to Verdun".' The battle continued for more than five months after Joffre wrote his Order of the Day. About one million soldiers died, roughly half German and half French. The soldier of the postcard is suitably battle-torn and appropriately defiant with his Lebel and bayonet.

31.

32.

33. This card of flags and flowers and its legend of 'Symbol of Victory' was obviously printed early in 1916 rather than at the end of the year. The slaughter of the battle of Verdun was still to take place and victory was a long way off.

34. A French salute to the Belgian Army, which throughout the war fought on the far left flank of the Allied line. The illustration shows, on the left, uniforms of former times, and on the right the 'new uniform'. This is a puzzle because the soldier shown here is British in every way – uniform, weapon, stance and expression. The only concession to Belgian uniform is the roundel type badge on the cap, which is not British. Belgian soldiers wore black leather leggings. The inset is King Albert of the Belgians.

33.

34.

Our Brave Allies – the French

35. A second French tribute to 'The valiant Belgians', in this case an officer with two NCOs and a French 75mm cannon, which the Belgian army used. The uniforms have been coloured with appalling crudity.

35.

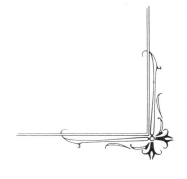

36. This is one of the most elaborate cards of the war, though the written message is brief enough. *My dear Jeanne, from Mezier. I send you a thousand kisses. Your dear friend who loves you for life. Joseph.* The card appears to refer to officers at a French military school, for on the left are cuirassiers or dragoons and on the right, infantry. Labelled 'The Class Thermometer', the card indicates, through the thermometer, practically a year's training. Around the edge of the thermometer's stand is 'Watch my temperature. With a pen make the black colour climb to the month you have chosen.' For October: 'I have — more days'. November: — more days'.

December: 'One month that will end in — days'. January: 'So many days left'. February: 'Still 260 meals'. March: 'Only — days'. April: 'In so many days I will be liberated'. May: '130 days left'. June: 'Still — days'. July: 'It's nearly finished'. August: 'Only five days left'. September: 'The end'. N.I.N.I. is a French expression used when studies are finished. Nini is also a girl's name. Across the bulb of the thermometer Joseph has written, *The warmer the sun gets the higher the temperature will climb.* A few aspects of the drawing are unclear. For instance, the infantrymen appear to be hiding from their cavalry colleagues.

36.

CHAPTER FIFTEEN

'Gallant Little Belgium' and Devoted Russians

The part played in the Great War by the Belgian Army is generally not mentioned in British and French histories, other than as a throwaway reference such as 'the Belgians held the left flank'. The war in the West was directly caused by the German invasion of Belgium and this little country's soldiers fought well and suffered bloodily. About 40,000 Belgian troops were killed, a large number from a national population of only four million.

British card producers rarely used Belgian images but propagandists assiduously exploited them in posters and press releases. Common slogans included 'The rape of Belgium', 'Gallant little

Belgium' and 'Poor little Belgium'. Belgium was presented, not inaccurately, as the innocent and virtually defenceless victim of a bully, Kaiser Wilhelm's Germany.

If the Belgians produced many war postcards it is not now apparent; even official archives contain relatively few examples. The scarcity of Belgian cards is understandable since the greater part of Belgium was under German occupation. In that part of the country which was free, West Flanders, soldiers and civilians used French and sometimes British cards. Those Belgian-subject cards which were published are interesting.

If the Russians had postcards during the Great War they did not reach the West, but British card producers were determined that

.Russian soldiers should not be left out of the public eye. Here are three examples of the Russians as seen by two British artists.

World War I in Postcards

1. Produced in France, this card shows King Albert firing a rifle at German soldiers in August 1914. From the large number of spent cartridges at his feet, he seems to have done some enthusiastic shooting. It is certainly possible that King Albert took some pot-shots, but Belgian military historians say that his officers would never have allowed him to get into a position which placed him in danger. That the card was intended for wide circulation is shown by the use of English and Russian as well as French for the caption.

2. One of the earliest postcards to show Belgian troops in action. During the German onrush in August–September 1914 they fought one delaying action after another behind barricades in the streets of innumerable towns.

LE ROI ALBERT

Par le sceptre et par le fusil.
A King, by sceptre, and by arms.
М. Ромбергъ. Король Альбертъ въ траншеѣ.

VISÉ PAR
2357.
I. M.

1.

1914... Troupes Belges barricadées dans les rues d'Alost essuyant le feu de l'ennemi

Belgian troops barricaded in the streets of Alost bearing the enemy's fire

2.

3.

3. The River Yser, which marked the left flank of the Allied front, ran through a sea-level coastal plain which had an elaborate system of artificial drainage. Threatened by overwhelming German forces, the Belgians breached the protective dykes and flooded the land. German troops, and some Belgians, were drowned and the region became impassable. Much equipment was lost, such as the heavy gun shown here. Even with its wheels fitted with large wooden 'shoes' it could not be dragged through the mud. To defend themselves by flooding the land the Flemish people of this area of Belgium sacrificed many homes and farms.

4. Also published in Paris, this card was a much too extravagant attempt to show the Belgian royal couple involved directly in the fighting. Queen Elizabeth of the Belgians did not need this type of unrealistic fiction to illustrate her undoubted devotion to her people. Precisely what she was doing for the wounded soldier is not clear. The king, map in hand and attended by a staff officer, seems to be unsure which road his cavalry should follow.

GUERRE 1914-1915. — Les Souverains héroïques. — Le Roi des Belges au front de ses armées et la Reine Elisabeth prodiguant ses soins aux blessés. — The heroic sovereign The King of Belgium at the front of his armies with the Queen Elisabeth attending to the wounded — L.L.
Paris n° 529

4.

5. The French artist Plument calls this drawing 'Le Culte du Drapeau' – the cult of the flag. The town of Dixmuide, on the Yser river, has been shelled by the Germans and its people and defenders are retreating to safety. Some, alas, have been killed. A wounded woman who was being wheeled to safety has died and been abandoned. This is a postcard of the winter of 1914.

6. This painting by A. Bastien was published in Brussels in 1914, while the Germans were occupying the city. Since the German authorities did not permit the publication of material which might be considered defamatory to them, the artist had to choose a 'safe' subject. He shows the channel at Nieuport, on the Allied left flank, and a military ambulance whose horses have been killed. Wounded men are to be seen crossing the bridge. On the card's reverse Bastien calls his painting 'Panorama de la bataille de l'Yser' – Panorama of the Battle of the Yser.

5.

6.

'Gallant Little Belgium' and Devoted Russians

7. Belgian soldiers exchange New Year greetings with their British comrades. The British soldier in the forefront is wearing a warm but non-issue fur garment for the dead of winter. Unusually, the legend is shown in Flemish as well as English and French. Although the war in Belgium was fought entirely in Flemish-speaking Western Flanders between January 1915 and September 1918, postcard publishers rarely used the Flemish language. The Flemish people considered this an affront to their language.

1918
COMRADES IN ARMS
FRÈRES D'ARMES, A Happy New Year. WAPEN BROEDERS.
Une Bonne Année, Gelukkig Nieuwjaar.

7.

1. No less an artist than Caton Woodville thought it worthwhile to glorify Russian soldiers. He may have had source illustrations which showed men of this stamp – élite Guardsmen, perhaps. They are all tall, well-built and well-equipped. Most Russian soldiers were poorly clad and ill-equipped. Entitled 'Russian prayer for success before combat', the card was published by Hildesheimer of London. ZEPTO paid for the embossed advertisement. Other makers of well-known products, such as Bovril, paid for similar advertisements.

1.

2. A. Pearson, who illustrated this act of bravery, provided the details which are printed on the reverse. 'One of the soldiers of a Russian regiment performed an act of great bravery, going out and rescuing a wounded comrade under the enemy's fire. The soldier was afterwards discovered to be a young woman who had joined as a volunteer. She was subsequently wounded and sent to the hospital at Kieff.' Several similar stories about women warriors were apocryphal but this one may have been true.

2.

RESCUING A WOUNDED COMRADE UNDER FIRE

'Gallant Little Belgium' and Devoted Russians

3. Another typical Pearson drawing. This is the story which accompanies it: 'This young soldier was working a field gun under what was described as a hellish rain of shrapnel. One by one his comrades fell but this youthful gunner did not flinch. Although wounded in the hand and neck he stuck to his post until reinforcements came to his aid. "Now I am not ashamed to die", he exclaimed and after bursting into tears he lost consciousness. He has been decorated with the Order of St. George for his bravery.'

3.

NOT ASHAMED TO DIE

CHAPTER SIXTEEN

American Cousins

The United States entered the war on the Allied side in April 1917, although a year was to elapse before American soldiers went into action. Their presence and their potential weight of numbers did however, give the European Allies new hope and the Germans a new dread. Masses of fresh, eager troops would obviously have a decisive effect on the outcome of the war.

From early in the war the British and French knew that they had American political support, and economic aid steadily increased. But many leaders realised that the most pressing need was for fit men to reinforce and perhaps take over from the exhausted European Allies and their Dominions. Various attempts were made to persuade the United States to declare war on Germany and take an active fighting part in the conflict. The sinking of the S.S. Lusitania in 1915 by a German U-boat and the consequent loss of 128 American lives, together with evidence of German complicity in a plot with Mexico to start a war against the United States in 1917, were steps in a process which finally brought the Americans into Europe. Before this some British postcards

concerning the United States were satirical and hostile.

American cards concerning American involvement are revealing. They show, for instance, a mixture of brashness, bravado and determination. New to war naturally the US armed forces were ill-informed about the hideous nature of the fighting in Europe, and they made no secret of their belief that their British and French Allies could have managed the conduct of the war differently. They felt that things would now improve and that their arrival would boost the morâle of the exhausted Allies.

Indeed, the Americans fought with great courage but they sustained needlessly high casualties because they had not learnt from the bitter experiences of their Allies during more than three years of war.

Interestingly, American postcards did not cover the humourous aspects of the war, as did the other Allies. Americans – publishers, artists, soldiers and public – took the war seriously. The British might laugh at some facet of training and even find humour on the battlefield, as Bruce Bairnsfather showed, but the

Americans perhaps either did not think of this side to the conflict or recoiled from it.

Statistics show us the significance of the American involvement. In April 1918 about 2,000 American troops joined the British Empire armies in the defence of Amiens. From then on the numbers involved rapidly increased. Between 9–15 June, 27,500 Americans helped to repulse a German advance and recaptured Belleau Wood. Between 18 July and 6 August 270,000 US troops played a major part in the first Allied advance of 1918. On 8 August, 54,000 of them fought with the British in the Somme advance, the number increasing to 108,000 by 19 August. On 12 September 550,000 Americans moved forward to capture 16,000 Germans and 443 guns. Between 26 September and 11 November no fewer than 1,200,000 Americans took part in the major final advance. As the Germans had feared and the European Allies had hoped, the fresh weight from across the Atlantic was decisive. The United States lost 48,909 men killed in battle and another 62,000 died of influenza during the epidemic which raged through Europe in 1918–19.

American Cousins

1. This tough Donald McGill card summed up European impressions of the Americans in 1916. They wanted the Germans beaten but were unwilling to become involved in the fighting themselves. The European Allies compared their own suffering with American affluence and security. McGill's American was not really a caricature but an impression of the perceived American personality and attitudes. It was published by Inter-Art Co. of London in its 'The Front' series.

2. This card, produced in France in the Lafayette Series, shows the Americans at the threatening stage of their war involvement. The reverse carries the message: *To Jackie from Daddy, France Mar. 1918*

SAY, I'M NEUTRAL AN' I DONT CARE A DARN WHO LICKS THE GERMANS!!

Moi, j'suis neutre, et j'm'en fous qui rosse les Allemands!

En voilà assez, j'entre aussi dans la partie.
I've stood their blarny long enough. I'll show what I mean.

1.

2.

3. Young America has arrived in France and merely has to be pointed in the right direction to begin his war. Miss France is happy to oblige. The French version is: 'The Boche, please?' In English this appears as 'Where are the Huns?' The Americans preferred this epithet. The publishers apparently also expected a market for the postcard in Russia. This is another card: *To Jackie from Daddy. France Feb. 1918*

Les Boches s. v. p.?
— La-bas!

Where are the Huns? — There!
Гдѣ пруссаки? — Тамъ!..

2680

3.

4. The British Empire and others would have been justified in taking offence at the depiction of the French flag as 'the Allies flag'. But the French were not responsible for this offence. The card was published by Patriotic Service Message and everything on it is in English. The reverse message is in French and is part of a longer correspondence spanning several other cards sent at the same time.

The Stars and Stripes
And the Allies flag too,
In company they wave
Till the War is through

4.

American Cousins

5. Inter-Art, London, expressed the expectations of Europeans – that no fewer than ten million American troops would come to Europe. In fact, the US Army had shipped 1,500,000 troops to Europe before the war ended and many more were in training at home. The White House and Capital Hill, Washington, emphasise the American decision to enter the war.

6. One of 312 postcards issued by the YMCA Hut Fund. This one was sent to Mr J. Denny, Priory Farm, Galgrave, near Diss, Norfolk. *Dear Jack, the restrictions having been taken off Pork you are at liberty to send as many as you like yours truly with best wishes Albert.* Pork what? Chops? The trench-raid training shown here may have given the Americans the impression that dealing with German soldiers was easier than it turned out to be.

5.

The emblem of Freedom, and ten millions to keep it flying!"

L'emblême de l'Indépendance, et dix millions d'hommes pour le tenir haut et ferme!

AMERICANS AT BAYONET PRACTICE ON THE PLAINS OF FRANCE.

6.

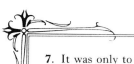

World War I in Postcards

7. It was only to be expected that American soldiers would be as homesick as other soldiers a long way from home. Bamforth did well with their six-part 'Down Texas Way' series.

7.

DOWN TEXAS WAY (1)
I can picture a spot so fair,
Smiling faces are ev'rywhere;
Wish some fairy would take me there,
And drop me nice and comfy in an old
arm-chair.

By permission of The Star Music Publishing Co. Ltd., London.

BAMFORTH (copyright.)

American Cousins

8. This classic Doughboy sketch was issued by the US Armed Forces and sent free through the mails. The drawing, by Marshall Davis, shows the casual but determined nature of the Americans. The rifle is the Garand.

8.

WE'RE NOT FOOLING

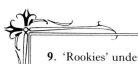

9. 'Rookies' under instruction by a tough Marine sergeant. Another Marshall Davis sketch for the US Army.

9.

HUT! - TEW - THREE - FOUR

CHAPTER SEVENTEEN

Field Service Postcards

All the armies involved in the Great War supplied Field Service postcards to their men. This enabled even those soldiers with little inclination to write letters, and those who lacked the ability to do so, to maintain some form of contact with their people at home. The British card provided the soldier with a limited choice of printed comments; he could stress those which seemed applicable at the time. The French and German cards allowed the soldier a little more freedom of expression. Field postcards gave the soldier a quick way to send a message to his family, who at least knew that their man was safe, or reasonably so, on the date shown on the card. These assurances would mean a lot while casualties continued to mount on such a massive scale. These service postcards were sent post free.

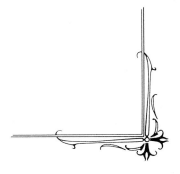

World War I in Postcards

1. The standard British Field Service Post Card, millions of which were used. The soldier could cross out sentences but add nothing more than dates and his signature. Many thousands of soldiers added other material, despite orders not to do so, and these cards were destroyed. While the cards were sent post free from the front, the Army warned addressees that when responding they must put stamps on their letters and cards.

2. The French military postcard could also be used by civilians but rarely was. The message was written on the reverse.

NOTHING is to be written on this side except the date and signature of the sender. Sentences not required may be erased. If anything else is added the post card will be destroyed.

I am quite well.

I have been admitted into hospital
{ *sick* } *and am going on well.*
{ *wounded* } *and hope to be discharged soon.*

I am being sent down to the base.

I have received your { *letter dated* _____
{ *telegram „* _____
{ *parcel „* _____

Letter follows at first opportunity.

I have received no letter from you
{ *lately*
{ *for a long time.*

Signature
only }

Date _____

[Postage must be prepaid on any letter or post card addressed to the sender of this card.]

1.

CORRESPONDANCE MILITAIRE

CARTE POSTALE

À L'USAGE DU CIVIL OU DU MILITAIRE
Ce côté est exclusivement réservé à l'adresse.

Expédiée par _____

Corps d'armée _____ Div.
Régiment _____
Bataillon _____ Escadron _____
Compagnie _____ Batterie _____
Section _____
Etat-Major _____
Quartier général _____
Service _____

FRANCHISE POSTALE

L'UNION FAIT LA FORCE

Pour la destination, à **un Militaire**, consulter l'affiche apposée dans les bureaux de poste et mairies.
à **un Civil**, le militaire remettra cette carte au vaguemestre.

2.

Field Service Postcards

3. A second type of army postcard, intended to do nothing more than inform the addressees of the sender's current address. On the reverse is a war loans exhortation, 'Envoyez des munitions!' – 'Send munitions!' Users of the card are told not to give details of military operations or the cards would not be sent.

3.

4. A German Feldpostkarte, sent by a Musketeer to a brother in a Guards Fusilier Regiment, in 1917. *I am healthy and in good spirits. Hope you are the same. We have good weather.* *Hope you have good weather too. Otherwise nothing new. Many greetings from your brother Emil.* The message is so banal that perhaps it contains a family code.

4.

CHAPTER EIGHTEEN

German Postcards

Allied war propaganda depicted the German troops as barbarians capable of the most hideous atrocities. It was alleged that they raped the women of Belgium and of occupied France, skewered babies on bayonets and boiled down the corpses of dead enemy soldiers to recover the fat, which was then used in candles.

One of the hideous atrocities alleged against the Germans was that priests were tied inside church bells while still alive and used as clappers for ringing the bells until they died. This particular story varied according to the public for whom the propaganda was intended. Sometimes the victims were said to be Canadian or Scottish soldiers.

The boiling down of corpses for fat and the use of men as bell clappers were propagandists' fantasies but many people were only too prepared to believe the worst of the Germans.

No act was supposedly too evil for them to perpetrate – according to 'reliable sources' and 'victims' own stories'. Small wonder then that the Germans were quickly dubbed Huns, recalling the barbarous Germanic tribes of more than a thousand years earlier. Most stories of atrocities were untrue, but the Germans played into the hands of the British and French propagandists with certain well-known acts of ruthless oppression and retaliation. The execution of Nurse Edith Cavell on charges of spying for the British in Belgium was their worst mistake. 'Remember Nurse Cavell' and 'Avenge Edith Cavell' became fighting slogans.

Like soldiers of all occupying armies before them, those who served the Kaiser were guilty of some cruel acts but they were nothing compared with the callous brutes of the following generation who formed Hitler's infamous SS units.

The great majority of the German troops of World War I avowedly fought, as did the British, for 'God, King (Kaiser) and Country'. Like the British and French, they were swept along by patriotism and nationalism and by the propaganda which told them that they were victims of the imperialistic British and the rapacious French.

German postcards were not unlike those of the Western allies in design and sentiment, except that they rarely showed humour. The

Germans saw nothing 'funny' about army life; service for the Fatherland was deadly serious. The British emphasis on humour in the midst of battle – as in Bruce Bairnsfather's 'Old Bill' drawings – was incomprehensible to the Germans. Even 'Scenes from Tommy's Life', cards which showed recruits being harassed by sergeant-majors, would not have been echoed in German military experience.

However, love and romance, family and children, courage and fortitude, all found ready and frequent reference in German postcards. British and French soldiers would have been astonished to find that the 'beastly Hun' had human qualities after all.

Their letters show them to be no less sensitive, afraid, anxious and loving towards their families than were their enemies of the battlefield.

German Postcards

1–6. This set of cards, under the general title of 'All My Happiness', show a great deal of romantic passion but, interestingly, they never directly refer to the war or even to the soldier's way of life.

1. All my happiness rests in you alone,
All my burning desires are centred on you,
And my noble thoughts.

2. All my happiness rests only in you,
Loveliest of all creatures,
Ever since you shared my life
Have I felt reborn.

All mein Glück
All mein Glück ruht nur in Dir,
Nur um Dich sich ranken
Meine heißen Wünsche all,
Meine Hochgedanken.

2.

All mein Glück
All mein Glück ruht nur in Dir,
Lieblichstes der Wesen,
Seit Du mir zur Seite bist
Fühl' ich mich genesen.

1.

3. All my happiness rests only in you
Most splendid of women,
Since through you I was allowed to see
The heavenly light.

4. All my happiness rests only in you,
Could one who possessed the happiness
of your love ever forget?

All mein Glück
All mein Glück ruht nur in Dir,
Herrlichste der Frauen,
Hab' ich doch durch Dich vermocht
Himmelslicht zu schauen.

3.

All mein Glück
All mein Glück ruht nur in Dir,
Könnte je vergessen,
Wer das Glück der Liebe hat,
Deiner Lieb' besessen?

4.

5. All my happiness rests only in you,
Rests in your love,
Every day I pray to God,
And ask that it remain throughout
eternity.

6. All my happiness rests only in
you,
All my burning desire
Is sanctified in you forever,
To you, the spring of beauty.

5.

6.

7. This postcard is uncannily similar to French cards of the same type. Even the design, with the soldier thinking of his sweetheart, who is shown in cameo, is strikingly similar. With his stout Mauser rifle, the soldier is defending his homeland. The verse reads:

'I stand in the darkness of midnight.
She still loves me, she is true to me,
Therefore I am happy and in a good
mood,
My heart beats warmly in the cold of
the night,
When it thinks about the love so far
away.'

Ich hatt' einen Kameraden.   Gez. W. Plauck.

8.

7.

200

German Postcards

8. Jackbooted German soldiers march away to war, accompanied down the street by loved ones. The crying baby and the sad young wife were constant symbols in German postcards. The card was posted on 23 April 1916 by a soldier of the 47th Reserve Division. The card carries the title of a song, 'Der gute Kamerad' – 'The Good Comrade'. The verse reads:

> I had a comrade,
> A better one you could not find.
> The drum was beaten for the battle.
> He marched alongside me
> Always in the same step.
>
> A bullet flew in our direction,
> Is it meant for me, is it for you?
> He was snatched away by it.
> He is lying in front of my feet
> As if he were part of myself.
>
> Reach out your hand to me,
> While I am inviting you:
> 'I can't give you my hand,
> May you remain in eternal life
> My good comrade!

In their sadder moments, German soldiers sang 'The Good Comrade'.

9. The archetypal military hero, wounded, his comrade dead, stands firm in battle against his enemies. The message reads: 'Thy kingdom come; Thy will be done, on earth as it is in heaven'. Many an Allied soldier of the war would have considered the use of the Lord's Prayer on a German postcard blasphemous. This card is from the Das Vaterunser series – 'Fur Vaterland and Recht', 'For Fatherland and Right'.

9.